Advance Praise for *Pr*

"Kathy is a leader I trust completely. Her work is so vital, so needed in our current landscape as the church struggles to navigate a path forward that is healthy and life giving and truly an embodiment of good news. Tender, weary, disoriented ones take heart: here is your pastor. Kathy is a faithful companion to those who wander, stumble, and, against all odds, continue to hope."

—Sarah Bessey, author of *Jesus Feminist* and
Miracles and Other Reasonable Things

"Kathy Escobar has that rare and brilliant gift of being able to x-ray our lives and to give words to our fears, pains, and longings so that we can see them clearly. *Practicing* is both deeply moving and incredibly insightful. I know it will be both a place of refuge and a catalyst for transformation for those fortunate enough to read it. The world has never been more in need of a book like this—and Kathy is the only one who could have given it to us."

—John Pavlovitz, author of *A Bigger Table*

"I love *Practicing: Changing Yourself to Change the World*. It's practical and easy to read, deep and full of wisdom. And it's for everybody who isn't perfect and doesn't live in a perfect world—religious or not, spiritual or not, churchy or not. If you're perplexed and weary (or fired up and ready to go) and don't know where to focus your attention and energy, this is the next book you should read."

—Brian D. McLaren, author, speaker, and activist

"I don't go to Kathy for the latest social justice hot take. I go to her to learn how to translate meaningful ideas into meaningful action—to move from speaking truth to living out the truth in sustainable ways among the complicated realities of human lives intersecting one another. She never promises quick fixes but advocates for the slow labor of *practicing* in the direction of justice. She lives this stuff, as you'll see inside the pages of this book, and she lit the road so that we can travel on it together."

—Cindy Wang Brandt, author of *Parenting Forward: How to Raise Children with Justice, Mercy, and Kindness*

"Kathy Escobar understands that the call toward authentic living is sacred and holy and for the greater good. In *Practicing: Changing Yourself to Change the World*, she shares the wisdom of her journey with fellow travelers who dare to take the road less traveled. Her clear and cogent guide is the kind of companion we all need as we practice generous living in these turbulent times."

—Paula Stone Williams, TED speaker and advocate for gender equity

"There are few people who live so fully, so thoughtfully, so serenely as Kathy Escobar. Now she has written a marvelous guide to help the rest of us do the same. A wise and gracious primer on life in the Spirit."

—Philip Gulley, Quaker pastor and author of *If the Church Were Christian*

"In an era of world history where the word *Christian* has become synonymous with theological debate, social inaction, and discrimination, *Practicing* emerges as a healing balm, offering a practical guide for people of faith to reconnect with our faith not just on a pious or intellectual level but in a way that impacts every aspect of our lives. With winsomeness, insight, and practical teaching, Escobar guides us on a path that will breathe new life into our faith and cause Christians to become a people who not only believe but also embody good news to ourselves, to others, and to the world around us. If you're ready for a spiritual renewal, read this book!"

—Brandan Robertson, lead pastor of Missiongathering San Diego and author of *The Gospel of Inclusion: A Christian Case for LGBT+ Inclusion in the Church*

"Changing ourselves to change the world inspires me. I love the way that Kathy calls us not just to personal reflection and action but also to community action. Kathy's diverse experience and her willingness to be vulnerable provide a unique and enriching approach to spiritual practices that is refreshing to read and compelling to apply to our lives. This is a very important book for all who want to grow in faith and deepen their intimacy with God."

—Christine Aroney-Sine, contemplative, activist, author of *The Gift of Wonder*, and facilitator of Godspacelight.com

"Kathy Escobar's book is a welcomed work, especially now when so many good people are overwhelmed with bad things happening in the world. Kathy's concern for seeing healthy values translated into effective action is evident not only in her own life but also in the lives of the communities she's associated with. Each chapter is so deep, informative, and helpful. But at the end of each chapter, she helps us render it into everyday living. What a great resource for personal transformation, community development, and world change!"

—David Hayward, the NakedPastor

"Amid the chaos of a deeply divided world, as well as churches that have conflated the good news with the illusion of the American dream, there has risen a heart-wrenching cry for love, dignity, and genuine belonging. Kathy Escobar hears and responds with hard-won wisdom that is pastoral, humble, and refreshingly honest. Drawing deeply from her Christian roots, she teaches practices that are not only well researched but have been well honed through the beautiful 'everyday' of real life with real people. If you want to learn more about what love looks like, read this book. If you want to become a lover of human souls, read this book. If you want to create a community of love, read this together. While it will certainly bring some discomfort, I am convinced that what Kathy Escobar offers is the most gospel-oriented,

practical book on personal and communal transformation that exists today."
— Ellen Haroutunian, psychotherapist, Benedictine oblate, and spiritual director

"Escobar is a gem as a teacher and writer. You will leave this book better than when you picked it up. Every individual and every faith community will benefit from the lessons on these pages. This is an important piece of work for anyone who interacts with those on the margins of society (which is to say everyone), and the chapter on grief alone is worth the cost of the book."
— Jerry Herships, pastor and author of *Rogue Saints* and *Last Call*

"A good book delivers on its promise, and this book does just that—challenging us to explore questions of faith that refuse to find satisfaction in a pithy response. We are invited to explore and venture out of our comfort zones to practice and dare to change. *Practicing* does not raise a ruckus and leave us hanging like an unscrupulous contractor who vanishes halfway through a major home renovation project. Instead, it allows for our fear of change while refusing to bow to the relentless pressure to stay small and safe. Kathy provides us a map and, perhaps most importantly, permission—permission to try, to fall down, and to rise and permission to have a little faith. What a great book!"
— Teresa McBean, copastor at Northstar Community and Executive Director of the National Association for Christian Recovery

"*Practicing* reminds us how much we need one another and how much we need to see what is *right* with us. This book nudges us all closer to ourselves, to each other, and to God by outlining simple spiritual practices. It is an essential guide for transformation in the messy and beautiful."
— Jan Shegda, PCC, IEA Accredited Professional, founder of Clarity Coaching, and Enneagram teacher

"I trust Kathy's heart because I have seen her practice what she preaches. Now she breaks open and preaches—in the best way—what she has been practicing for so many years. I, for one, need to take off perfectionism and lean into the grace and wisdom of these practices. This is a beautiful, humble, wise, and world-changing book."
—Idelette McVicker, founder of *SheLoves* magazine

"What a joy to find including, equalizing, mourning, and failing (failing!) on a list of spiritual practices alongside the traditional practices of prayer, meditation, service, and fasting found in thousands of other works on the topic. *Practicing* cuts through the traditional theological arguments and trendy spiritual experiments and offers a path for walking out the core principles of embodied faith in a way that is holistic, sustainable, satisfying, and fruitful. In *Practicing*, Kathy Escobar has given hope and a practical path to those of us who long to make our faith a verb for the sake of the world as well as our own souls."
—Phyllis Mathis, spiritual mentor and cocreator of Walking Wounded: Hope for Those Hurt by Church

"Kathy Escobar is a true doer of the Word, not just a hearer only. She brings her pastoral heart to everything she does, including this latest offering, which is a true gift to all of us who are seeking to follow Jesus and not just be a fickle fan."
—Steve Roach Knight, cofounder of Transform Network

"Personal and collective transformation is foundational to creating just and healthy systems in society. And practices are foundational to that change. Kathy brilliantly and compellingly invites us on a journey of transformation through ten practices, which, as she illustrates, are foundational for those wanting to effect change in our increasingly complex world. She has a unique capacity to see the systems of injustice and both to articulate practices for those who hold power and privilege in the systems and to daily be in practice as a learner with those who have been oppressed by the same system. Kathy takes us to the depths of our souls and provides practical steps for growth and action, while holding the complexity and mystery. And she always leaves us with hope!"

—Pamela Wilhelms, founder of Wilhelms Consulting Group and the Soul of the Next Economy Initiative

Practicing

Practicing

Changing Yourself to Change the World

KATHY ESCOBAR

WJK WESTMINSTER JOHN KNOX PRESS LOUISVILLE • KENTUCKY

First edition
Published by Westminster John Knox Press
Louisville, Kentucky

20 21 22 23 24 25 26 27 28 29—10 9 8 7 6 5 4 3 2 1

Book design by Drew Stevens
Cover design by Mary Ann Smith

Library of Congress Cataloging-in-Publication Data is on file at the Library of Congress, Washington, DC.

ISBN: 978-0-664-26584-7

For Jose, my faithful and true and solid rock.
For Josh, Julia, Jamison, Jonas, and Jared,
you give me faith for the future.
Jared, we will miss you forever, but we'll keep doing our best
to "change someone else's world."
And for The Refuge, my beloved community,
There's no one I'd rather practice with.

CONTENTS

Acknowledgments   ix
Introduction: Practice   1

1. The Practice of Healing   11
2. The Practice of Listening   31
3. The Practice of Loving   49
4. The Practice of Including   71
5. The Practice of Equalizing   93
6. The Practice of Advocating   119
7. The Practice of Mourning   139
8. The Practice of Failing   161
9. The Practice of Resting   183
10. The Practice of Celebrating   201

Conclusion: Keep Practicing   217
Notes   227

ACKNOWLEDGMENTS

It takes a village to write a book, and it takes an even bigger village to hold a mommy up when her child dies while her newest book is in production. My family is living out paradox in its purest form—contradicting things together in the same space. While a bomb went off in our hearts and we're mourning the death of our nineteen-year-old son, Jared, we're also celebrating the birth of *Practicing* into the world, a project all my kids have been supportive of since its inception. Jared was a phenomenal leader and social justice advocate, and his belief in this book and the need for embodying change by changing ourselves will help me carry on. One of his most well-known sayings was "You can't change the world, but you can change someone else's world."

There are so many people who made this project possible. If it weren't for the faithful and fun presence of my husband, Jose, most of my dreams would still be dreams. He is an amazing teammate, cheerleader, and solid rock. My young adult kids—Josh, Julia, Jamison, and Jonas— are excellent cheerleaders, too. Their "Go Mom!" texts kept me going. It's also important for me to acknowledge my mom, Karen Silveira, who turned eighty as I finished this manuscript and still does so many things to support our work and family week after week.

I also want to thank all my teammates at The Refuge, but especially Mike Herzog and Marrty Dormish, who make room for me to focus when I have thousands of tasks that need to get done; their patience and steadfast support is a true gift. Without the wisdom and encouragement of my agent, Rachelle Gardner, I don't think I would have tackled another book, and without the eyes and hearts of Stacy Schaffer, Sage Harmos, Mark Votava, and Kathe Kokolias, *Practicing* wouldn't be what it became. We really do need advocates that inspire and strengthen us. Last, I want to honor the circle of love and support I always feel from The Refuge community; my women's, recovery, and faith-shift groups; and online and real-life friends who share their stories, cheer me on, and are living out these practices in such tangible and beautiful ways. Life is meant to be practiced together, and I have some pretty marvelous people to practice with.

INTRODUCTION

Practice

Prac·tice — *praktəs*
Verb / present participle: **practicing**
1. To participate in an activity or implement a skill repeatedly to develop greater proficiency
2. To intentionally work toward growth through repetition and experience

An ounce of practice is worth more than tons of preaching.
— Mahatma Gandhi

In my life as a pastor, blogger, advocate, and friend, each week I have multiple conversations with people of all shapes, sizes, and experiences about issues of faith. Some are loyal church attenders, deeply dedicated to their local community. Others are what I call *faith-shifters*, people who have deconstructed former beliefs and aren't sure what they believe anymore. Still others fit in the categories of *Nones* and *Dones*, folks who are at a point in their lives where they have no clear spiritual tethering or are completely done with all things church. Some are young, with an enthusiasm and zest that is contagious, while others are older and genuinely tired after hacking at a life of faith for decades and not quite sure where it got them. Some end up crying in our conversation, feeling lost and disconnected from God, while others feel energized about working in their local community on behalf of justice and equality in these ever-changing times. Some identify as straight, others as LGBTQ+. Some are rich and others are living in poverty. Some have graduate-level education and others barely squeaked through high school. Some are married, and others are single. Some cringe when the word "church" comes up, and others joyfully talk about what they learned last Sunday.

Despite the vast array of differences, there is one consistent thread throughout all these conversations, week after week, month after month, year after year. It's a guiding story that everyone has in common: *an authentic desire to live out their faith in a tangible way.*

To love their neighbors
To make a difference
To embody the hands and feet of Jesus
To be braver in relationship
To practice faith, not just talk about it
To help make the world a better place

For the people who identify as spiritual refugees or church-burnouts, they have heard enough sermons to last a lifetime; they are completely done with going through the motions of organized religion, and most want nothing to do with the system anymore but have a deep longing to be a force for good in our hurting world. Those who regularly attend church consistently offer comments that describe an itch to cultivate a more practical faith and a less theoretical one. They share stories of a desire to serve and help others and offer Jesus' love in actions, not just words. They are realizing that real change in the world starts with their own lives first.

I understand that stirring. While I am a pastor, my work is in a messy and beautiful eclectic Christian community and mission center that is extremely untraditional. The core of our life together is relationship and practice. Really looking inside ourselves at our struggles, strengths, and weaknesses and then trying to live out of a new place with others around us is extremely tough to do! I sometimes miss the ease of my past experience—sitting in church, getting inspired through worship and a good sermon, and going home.

Yet something was deeply missing when life was like that. On the outside, I looked like a "good" Christian wife and mother, faithfully attending church, and following the unwritten rules of what I thought was a faithful life. Inside, I felt lonely, disconnected from my heart, afraid to show up more honestly out of fear. I didn't have any safe spaces to speak more honestly about some of my true struggles in my relationship with God and my own soul. I wasn't sure who I could trust and who I couldn't.

Thankfully, I ended up in a renegade women's small group in a conservative Baptist church that opened up my heart and head in a way that changed things forever. The group was incredibly unique, tucked out of sight from regular ministry programming in a system built on certainty. It was a brave space to be more honest, to share our real struggles, raw questions, and scary doubts, and to not be met with judgment, advice, or fixing. Instead, I was met with honesty and hope. The women shared some of the same crazy thoughts that were running through my head, and I felt much less alone. We were honest about our fear that maybe our efforts in faith were channeled in the wrong direction, that many of the unsaid Christian rules we were following weren't going to serve us well in our marriages, parenting, or communities.

I spent three years in that group, and it changed my life forever. I knew I could never go back to a Bible study that wasn't also talking about real life and honest struggles. I knew I couldn't spend any more time on conversations that remained stuck on picking apart particular Bible verses or who was right and who was wrong. I knew I needed to keep pushing out of my comfort zone and into the mess and muck of my own pain, the pain of others, and the pain of our unjust world. I knew I wanted to live out the ways of Jesus in a tangible way that transformed not only my soul but also my relationships and the wider world around me.

In a nutshell, I discovered the beauty of the word "practice." Real change in ourselves doesn't come through a few minor tweaks in our behavior or from breezing through a book on practice. Practice is centered on deep inner work in our souls that propels us to habitually, intentionally, and repeatedly live out new, healthier ways over the long haul. In God's economy, improvement isn't measured with words like *more, bigger,* or *better* but rather by what's *deeper, stronger,* and *more integrated.* Deeper, stronger, more integrated people help create deeper, stronger, more integrated systems. This only comes through practice and learning to live out something different over and over again.

Practice is also about engaging even when we are scared. Playing instead of sitting on the sidelines. Showing up in relationship instead of hiding. Sitting in hard places with people instead of avoiding pain. Listening to others who look, think, and believe differently than us instead of always talking. Allowing ourselves to be vulnerable as people of faith instead of protecting our hearts, money, and time. Practice is about making mistakes, getting our hands dirty, and giving ourselves and others heaps of grace. It's about getting out of our heads and into our hearts, guts, and souls. It's about putting feet to our faith. It's about loving God, our neighbors, and ourselves through actions not just words.

Practice remains one of my favorite words because the world needs more of it right now. In times of deep division, great change, and never-ending brokenness, we need brave people of practice to help us keep moving forward.

For far too long, our neighborhoods, our cities, our world has been crying out for hope while we Christians have been sitting around in our comfortably protected bubbles talking about theology.

Theology won't heal the world. Sure, theology informs us and is a powerful catalyst and reason why we do what we do. However, let's be honest. For the most part, the world has had enough of our theology. Many are sick and tired of watching Christians circle our wagons, separate from others, and fight against equality and freedom. They are hungry for healing, connection, help, touch, advocates, allies, and people who will sit with them in the dark.

The world is looking for peacemakers, bridge builders, dignity restorers, and people of presence.

Learning to be those kinds of people doesn't happen from going to church every Sunday week after week. It doesn't drop into our living room while we are sitting on the couch scrolling through social media or by listening to the latest, greatest podcast. *It comes through practice.* It comes through learning a better way than we've maybe been taught in the homes we grew up in or the churches we attended. It comes through flesh-and-blood relationships. Through real experience. Through stories. Through pain.

Over the years I have come to believe that faith is a verb. Verbs are action words, and God's spirit flows through people. It makes me think of the timeless words attributed to sixteenth-century mystic, Saint Teresa of Avila:

Christ has no body now but yours,
No hands, no feet on earth but yours,
Yours are the eyes with which he looks
Compassion on this world,
Yours are the feet with which he walks to do good,
Yours are the hands with which he blesses all the world.
Yours are the hands, yours are the feet,
Yours are the eyes, you are his body.
Christ has no body now on earth but yours.

When I read this piece aloud to different groups, I always like to change "yours" to "ours." *Christ has no body now on earth but ours. We are God's eyes, hands, and feet.*

Faith is not knowledge. It's not static. It's not a "thing" we can grasp. Rather, it's an act, occurrence, mode of being. It's a mix of actions that reflect God in us and through us. It's a myriad of *-ing* words that are active, tangible, and always in motion.

Faith is a verb.
It's meant to be practiced.

I've found that most people I know across ages and experiences—agnostics, faith-shifters, faithful followers of Jesus, and even folks from other faith traditions—nod their head in agreement when I say this out loud. Faith is a verb. Whether we're a millennial, baby boomer, Generation X, Y, Z or whatever new name they come up with next, most everyone's souls resonate with the idea that faith is meant to be lived out tangibly with other people. It's an action not an idea. It's a life of practice, not theory.

And it's something a lot of us need a little help with.

Many of us weren't taught a life of courageous practice in church. We know a lot about the Bible, about service to others, about showing up as Christians at church, but many have found that we know little when it comes to healthy relationship skills, social justice advocacy, or even knowing how to truly hold space for differences between people. We need tools, examples, and real-life stories that will help bring our desires to life. We need challenge, encouragement, and ideas. We need inspiration—from the Bible and from other wisdom books and teachers—that will fuel us when we're tired and desperately want to go back to the comforts of passivity. We need reminding that what we practice at the smallest level flows into the wider world and transforms it.

This is what *practicing* is all about. It's a book centered on practice that changes us so that we can be part of changing the world.

My hope is that as you journey through this book you feel encouraged and challenged and in the company of kindred spirits who are willing to engage in courageous practice, too. People who are done only going to church and want to *be* the church. Men and women who want to learn better ways of relating to themselves, others, and God than we may have been taught in our homes and Sunday school classes. Those who are hungry for a practical faith that connects our hearts and experience in flesh and blood, glory and pain, beauty and the mess.

I wish we could be in the same room together, sharing our failures and triumphs, our humble attempts at practice and our struggles together. Even though that's not possible, I'm going to pretend I'm processing these practices with you all in my living room, one of my favorite places for good conversations. Sometimes you are going to be irritated with me because some of these practices will make you extremely uncomfortable. You will start to wish for a book that doesn't require as much of you, where you can skim the words and gain a quick shot of inspiration instead. I'm just not that kind of person.

My work is about creating brave and safe spaces for transformation. We never change through comfort. We change through challenge, dissonance, disruption, and new stories. Trust me, I often want to flee back to comfort, too. The work of living out an honest, vulnerable, tangible faith requires parts of us we may not want to give.

While this book was in the final stages of production we received the brutal and heart-shattering news that our fifth child, one of our twins, Jared, took his own life in his dorm room just shy of his twentieth birthday. A paradoxical mix of influential outdoor education leader, excellent student and athlete, deep philosophical thinker, and creative inspiration to our family and countless Colorado kids, Jared's death has rocked not only our world but so many others, too. Crawling through unbearable grief and every parent's worst nightmare, I am now having to practice so much of what is in this book in far more deep, holy, and uncomfortable ways.

As you live into your own individual discomfort and personal stories of life and faith, I hope you can remain open and be challenged to engage and dive in as deeply as you are able. I also encourage you to use this material in your own way. Linger on one chapter for a long time, or work through it all at once. Each of us are in unique spaces in our spiritual journey, and it's important to own what is stirring up in you and what you might be called to consider. What I hope is that as we walk through this book together you practice openness, willingness, and possibility. I'm trying to practice these things right along with you.

Each chapter will be centered on an action or verb. These actions are core to an integrated life of courageous practice and include healing, listening, loving, including, equalizing, advocating, mourning, failing, resting, and celebrating. I've also included options for personal and group reflections at the end of each chapter, along with ideas for practices to experiment with and resources to dig deeper on your own. These are not exhaustive lists, but ideas that come from my own experience; consider other ones you would add as time goes on. If you decide to engage with *practicing* in a group, either online or in real life, I always recommend setting a few ground rules for your conversation before you start. These are possibilities:

Stick with "I" statements and your own story.
Maintain confidentiality.
Go around the room for some of the questions and make space to hear from everyone instead of only hearing the loudest voices. Give everyone freedom to pass.
Don't fix or offer unsolicited advice. Practice listening.

Honor the time with brevity, and keep your sharing to three to five minutes (or whatever time you decide depending on how many people you have in the group) to ensure that everyone has a chance to share. At least do one round of hearing from everyone before opening the conversation up to additional reflections. Otherwise, you may never hear from some participants in the group.

Whether you're engaging with this book alone or with others, the most important thing about *practicing* is to be creative and build on these ten practices in ways that work for you. These actions—applied and expanded differently in everyone's unique context—can bring transformation not only to us but to the wider world, too. Each of us can throw our stones into the water, making ripples that last far beyond what meets the eye.

Practicing is about creating ripples, making waves, catalyzing change.

It's centered on learning for people who want to be challenged in their relationships. It's about forward movement in our faith because looking back no longer holds the same value. It's about finding courage to dive deep and discover ways we can become better listeners, lovers, advocates, and friends.

You were drawn to this book for a reason. You are longing for something different. You are hungry. You are open to possibility. You are tired of talking and want to start doing. You are worn out by the division and fragmentation in faith, politics, and the never-ending news cycle and want to participate in cultivating healing. You are waking up to the deep grooves of racism and sexism that permeate our systems and know you need to do something about it.

Welcome. I am so glad you are here.

Faith is a verb.

Let's get practicing together.

CHAPTER 1

THE PRACTICE
OF HEALING

Heal—hēl
Verb / present participle: **healing**
1. To transform into greater wholeness
2. To bring relief and health to areas of distress and dissonance
3. To repair something that is broken

I suppose since most of our hurts come through relationship, so will our healing.[1]

—William Paul Young

The other day I got a long voice mail from an acquaintance who lives in another state. She is wrestling with difficult family members, the recent loss of her dad, and the realities of being a single mom with little to no extra support. She's tired and lonely. On her message she shared her current struggles and then added something that struck me because I'm not emotionally close with her: "Kathy, thank you for listening to me ramble. I have felt so alone, with no one to share these things with. Just having someone to say this stuff to on the other end of the phone is helping me heal."

Honestly, I haven't done much except listen and encourage from afar.

The sincerity of her words reverberated, especially since she has been a faithful Christian for many years, attending church regularly. All those years of going to church hasn't yielded the fruit she really needs right now—a space to share the *real* things that are going on in her life with *real* people. She's connecting with me on the phone, but really she wants a warm embrace from a friend, someone to look her in the eye, and remind her she's not alone.

This shouldn't be a stretch, but these kinds of spaces and places are, indeed, rare.

Church often centers on going to a place, singing songs, listening to a positive and challenging message from a pastor, and going home. We might hang out with a few others for small-group Bible study or serve together on a project, but for the most part many of us keep the inner workings of our personal life tucked away while outwardly projecting something different. This isn't true for all of us; I know some of you are in solid communities that foster a spirit of healing. I love knowing you have a healing space to keep working on ongoing transformation in your life. I also know some of you don't go to church anymore; for all kinds of reasons, it just stopped working for you.

Most times, when I hear people's painful stories for the first time, I ask, "Who else knows about this?" The response is usually the same: "No one."

"No one" always fractures my heart.

That was the story of my Christian life for many years, too. I was used to carrying my struggles and doubts on my own, grinding down to try to "figure it out" with God and myself, praying harder, working harder, and pretending I was doing much better than I really was. As I shared in the introduction, participating in that women's group over two decades ago changed everything for me, not just then but still today. It opened up a pathway to a much-needed practice as humans living in a broken world — *healing.*

Healing Starts with Ourselves

When you hear the word "healing," what do you think of?

Often, it's associated with healing of a disease, a miracle, an erasure of some sort of pain. Sometimes we think of it as a particular moment in time where what hurt doesn't anymore. In Christian circles, healing is often the release from the stronghold of addiction, the curing of a disease, the transition from a struggle to victory. Many I know speak of a spiritual healing they received when they turned their lives over to Jesus. I have also noticed that healing tends to be talked about as something for "those people who need more help because their lives are harder" or in the context of "they just need God's healing."

It's easier to think of healing as something that *someone else* needs more than *we* do.

However, like every single one of the practices Jesus calls us to, it starts with us first. It makes me think of some of the things he rattles off in the Gospels:

> "How can you say to your brother, 'Let me take the speck out of your eye,' when all the time there is a plank in your own eye?"
>
> Matt. 7:4 NIV

> "Blind Pharisee! First clean the inside of the cup and dish, and then the outside also will be clean."
>
> Matt. 23:26a NIV

> "Let anyone among you who is without sin be the first to throw a stone at her."
>
> John 8:7b

Most of us draw great hope from the simplicity of Jesus' words when he was asked, "'Which commandment is the first of all?'" (Mark 12:28). Jesus' answer: "The first is, 'Hear, O Israel: the Lord our God, the Lord is one; you shall love the Lord your God with all your heart, and with all your soul, and with all your mind, and with all your strength.' The second is this: 'You shall love your neighbor as yourself.' There is no commandment greater than these" (Mark 12:29–31). I love Jesus' words, but *I truly believe one of the reasons the world is so screwed up right now is that we are, indeed, loving our neighbors as ourselves.*

The problem is that a lot of us actually hate ourselves—and others notice it. Years ago I met with several master's level counseling students at a local university who considered themselves non-Christian, atheist, or agnostic. They needed to interview a Christian leader for one of their assignments, and one of their first questions was, "Why does almost every Christian we meet seem to hate themselves and think they are a miserable wretch? We just don't get it."

Hate is a strong word, I know, and I always told my kids not to use it. But self-hatred is also more prevalent than we like to admit. The more I intersect with people in the depths of their experience—Christian or not—the more I see the magnitude of people struggling to believe their value and worth. How many are wracked with self-loathing. How many are constantly trying to figure out ways to escape their pain. How many are using countless unhealthy self-protection mechanisms ranging from work to food to porn to drugs and alcohol to religion. *How many are deeply dedicated to helping others while subtly and silently hating and neglecting themselves.*

My friend Stacy knows a thing or two about self-hatred and pretending things are better than they really are. Raised in an atheist home, when she turned her life over to Jesus, she went all-in and soon was leading a thriving youth ministry and getting her master's degree in counseling at a seminary. Devout, strong, professional, with gorgeous brown hair and a megawatt smile, she appeared to be a model Christian. Yet, underneath she had an intense and tangled story of abuse, neglect, and deep woundedness. She buried it under the guise of "Jesus healing her." A consummate helper, she kept pushing down her own pain and tried to focus on others. In fact, she even moved to Colorado to "help" at The Refuge, the Christian community and mission center I co-pastor. She wasn't here for a month when she realized how her desire to love others was impeded by her lack of loving herself. When she started listening to others sharing honestly in our brave healing community, Stacy began to come apart and finally admitted the depth of her self-hatred and shame and acknowledged she desperately needed healing. She recently shared this with me, "For so long, 'Achieve, impress, and protect' was my mantra. I felt a low constant hum of always being exposed. Even though I often dreaded it, I kept showing up for healing groups and other spaces to grow in our community and began to slowly tell my own truth. Over time, I have become so much more free. The hum is gone, I can breathe, and I feel like a whole person for the first time in my life."

The practice of healing starts with ourselves.

We've All Got Work to Do

When we're honest, most of us want to skip over the hard work of healing in our own lives and help others do their work instead. We'd rather give than receive, do well than struggle, and let someone else spill their guts instead of sharing ours. It's safer and less uncomfortable. Yet, one of the most important practices we can embrace as part of our ongoing transformation is embracing and integrating our own story, with all its good, bad, and ugly.

Dr. Brené Brown, who has brought conversations about vulnerability, shame, and relational healing to the forefront for many in the past few years, says it well: "I now see how owning our story and loving ourselves through that process is the bravest thing that we will ever do."[2] She also nails it with this reminder of how we tend to default toward an unhealthy independence, trying to fix struggles on our own so we can remain safely protected.

One of the greatest barriers to connection is the cultural importance we place on "going it alone." Somehow we've come to equate success with not needing anyone. Many of us are willing to extend a helping hand, but we're very reluctant to reach out for help when we need it ourselves. It's as if we've divided the world into "those who offer help" and "those who need help." The truth is that we are both.[3]

Often, when we have extra margin and resources we see ourselves as the ones who can "help heal" those who struggle with poverty, mental illness, or addiction. We forget that we are equal strugglers together, no less or more than another. My friend Janice, who lives alone on a small monthly disability check and has suffered the ravages of chronic illness for years, isn't the person I *help*. She shares her story, and I share mine. I give her a ride, and she gives me some wisdom. I might look better on the outside, but inside we are the same—fragile, strong, messy, and beautiful human beings learning to love and be loved.

Accepting that we ourselves need help is a core practice of healing and transformation.
Over the past twenty years, I have facilitated countless workshops and groups centered on healing and recovery. I am always a participant, too, in the thick of my own healing journey and ever-reminded I'll be engaging in the practice of healing my entire life. I'm usually in good company. In fact, every time, in every group, no matter our socioeconomics, education, theology, age, or

circumstance, almost everyone shares the same reality—we always have healing work to do. There are always patterns to shift, change we hope for in our lives and relationships, and a desire for more meaningful connection with God, ourselves, and others. Many also express that there are few tangible tools to help us get there. Our families and churches—two of the primary spaces where we spend a lot of time—usually aren't that helpful in practicing a healthier way.

Healing always starts with getting more honest. Below is a list of unhealthy patterns in relationship. You may or may not identify with all of the items on the list, but if you're human, you can probably relate to a few. Read through and check which ones describe you at this point in your life, remembering some might need bigger checks than others. Walk through it any way that works for you, trying to be honest and reflective. Despite years of personal work, I still have boxes to check. Why? Because I'm human. You are, too.

When I'm honest, sometimes I:
- ☒ Isolate from community and friends.
- ❏ Live from a foundation of fear and am often scared to hope, try, love, connect.
- ☒ People please.
- ❏ Have consuming thoughts about how people view me.
- ❏ Caretake, putting everyone else's needs above my own.
- ❏ Struggle with perfectionism or "all or none" thinking, having no grace for mistakes.
- ❏ Feel low self-esteem—"I'm unworthy. I don't deserve better. I'm unlovable."
- ❏ Remain unaware of my own feelings.
- ❏ Refuse to apologize and hold on to grudges.
- ❏ Have unhealthy boundaries so people use or take advantage of me.
- ❏ Am unable to say "no" and mean it.
- ☒ Minimize or justify bad behavior of others around me.

❏ Swing between repressing my anger and letting it rip in unhealthy ways.

❏ Avoid pain by using some form of avoidance (alcohol, food, work, relationships, drugs, TV, social media).

❏ Take my negative feelings out on my kids or people closest to me.

❏ Feel paralyzed and unable to move forward on goals or change.

❏ Question and doubt my faith (but pretend like I don't).

Yikes! How did it feel to check some of these boxes? Did you want to find a way to justify or rationalize them? I know I did. There are many other things we could add to this list, but these seem to cover a solid range of relationship work a lot of us need for ongoing healing. We're not bad or unfaithful for struggling with these. They're part of the human experience. The practice of healing is about acknowledging our humanness and also being willing to develop better ways of moving in the world. Most of us didn't learn this in our families, traditional church, or college, so we're often left out on our own.

Part of an active, vibrant, tangible faith is becoming healthier human beings and learning to practice a better way.

Here's the good news—there is a better way. Also, it's not just for people who spend hundreds of dollars in therapy month after month. It's for everyone who wants to engage in the bloody, beautiful, messy work of practicing healing.

Read the items in the next list and mark them in two different ways. First, check the ones you're feeling pretty good about right now, areas of relationship where you are, indeed, practicing a better way. Next, go through and circle the ones where you know you still have some healing work to do.

I'm healing, practicing a better way by:

- ☐ Reaching out to friends or helpers in my community for love, prayer, and support.
- ☐ Doing hard things even when I am scared — pushing through fear so I'm not paralyzed.
- ☑ Living with others' disapproval instead of trying to fix it (this includes disgruntled kids who aren't happy about being disciplined or not getting their way).
- ☑ Practicing good self-care (space for fun, breaks, physical health).
- ☐ Giving myself grace when I make mistakes.
- ☐ Believing I am worthy of love and respect.
- ☐ Noticing my feelings, identifying, "I'm sad, mad, hurt, present, etc."
- ☒ Asking for forgiveness when I make a mistake and hurt someone.
- ☐ Saying "no" when I need to and living with the fallout.
- ☐ Expressing anger in a healthier way, through honest conversations, physical exercise, contemplative practices, or other creative expressions.
- ☐ Allowing myself to feel pain and let God and others in instead of avoiding it.
- ☐ Own my feelings and express them in a safe place.
- ☐ Taking one small step, no matter how tiny, to move forward and change.
- ☐ Sharing my honest feelings about God and faith without editing them.

Where were your areas of celebration? Places for growth?

The practice of healing is centered on being more honest about these things not only with ourselves, but with others as well. We need to remember this is a completely countercultural way of living, and there is always a cost to the ways of Jesus. The culture around us values success, strength, and power far more than honesty, humility, and vulnerability. This is why so many men and women feel extremely conflicted when it comes to a life of honesty.

My friend Mike lived a divided life for many years until his wife died and he began to get in touch with a lifelong sexual addiction. As he processed through that struggle, he uncovered a mountain of unhealthy relationship patterns he had learned in his family and church for many years. Slowly, surely, he began to address them, bring them into the light of healing community, and begin to practice a better way. I met him fifteen years ago, at the beginning of his journey. Watching how far he's come has been truly delightful, but it hasn't happened by magic. He shows up for recovery meetings regularly, asks for help, and embodies a humble way of being that is completely contrary to the stereotype of "strong Christian men." His weakness has made him strong; it reminds me of the words of the apostle Paul in 2 Corinthians 12 about reframing weakness. I especially like the *The Message* translation:

> Then [Jesus] told me, My grace is enough; it's all you need. My strength comes into its own in your weakness. Once I heard that, I was glad to let it happen. I quit focusing on the handicap and began appreciating the gift. It was a case of Christ's strength moving in on my weakness. Now I take limitations in stride, and with good cheer, these limitations that cut me down to size—abuse, accidents, opposition, bad breaks. I just let Christ take over! And so the weaker I get, the stronger I become.
>
> 2 Cor. 12:9–10

Unless we're willing to admit our weaknesses, we can never experience the strength of healing.

The Beatitudes and the Twelve Steps Work

I have been regularly attending Twelve Step meetings for over fifteen years now, mostly centered on codependency and untangling from unhealthy relationship patterns. I'm an adult child of an alcoholic, an Enneagram 2 (helper), and pastor. I have always outwardly thrived on being a caretaker, people-pleaser, and peacemaker. Inside, though, it's a different story, and years ago I knew I had to address these unhealthy patterns or I would pass them on to my five children and perpetuate my dysfunction in them. Each and every time I put my butt in the chair for any type of recovery meeting I do two things: (1) thank God for my kids who were a primary catalyst to enter recovery and (2) think to myself with a chuckle, "I wish more people would skip church and come here instead."

So much magic happens at recovery meetings! Others who are in recovery echo this sentiment, especially those who spent years attending church but never experienced healing from their real struggles. In conversations I have with faith deconstructors who are done with church but not God, they often repeat the same thing: "I really wish church were more like an AA meeting; then I might want to go again." While I know many churches are doing solid work in the area of healing and transformation in their communities, it's still fair to say that many congregations of all sizes and traditions could learn a lot from recovery meetings. There's something so beautiful about the simplest of experiences: Chairs in a circle, reading from a binder or a little blue book, awkward silence, and the true and honest words from people of all shapes, sizes, and experiences sharing their experience, strength, and hope. It is safe because it's real.

The Beatitudes, the words of Jesus at the beginning of the Sermon on the Mount, and the Twelve Steps gracefully dovetail into each other because they center on a much-needed ingredient for personal and community healing—an attitude of humility. These are the first five of a slightly modified version of the Twelve Steps that we read at our Refuge Recovery meeting.

1. Admitted we were powerless over our addictions and compulsive behaviors and that our lives had become unmanageable.
2. Came to believe that a Power greater than ourselves could restore us to sanity.
3. Made a decision to turn our will and our lives over to the care of God as we understood God.
4. Made a searching and fearless moral inventory of ourselves.
5. Admitted to God, to ourselves, and to another human being the exact nature of our wrongs.

In Matthew 5:3–12, known as the Beatitudes, Jesus reminds us that we're blessed and experience the kingdom of God when we are spiritually poor, willing to mourn, meek, merciful, hungry for justice, pure in heart, and peacemakers. When we live this way, we are changed. The Beatitudes, like the Twelve Steps, become core values and actions that propel us to embody a more integrated way of moving in the world. These practices shift significant things in our souls, not just our minds. The result: visible transformation that heals not only our own lives but others around us as well.

Daily I am reminded how contrary these ways of Jesus are to the ways of the world. In the same way, when I'm in healing meetings, I'm reminded of how contrary many of these meetings are to the ways of contemporary church. I love what Richard Rohr says in his rich, beautiful book about spirituality and the Twelve Steps called *Breathing Under Water*:

Christians are usually sincere and well-intentioned people until you get to any real issues of ego, control, power, money, pleasure, and security. Then they tend to be pretty much like everybody else. We are often given a bogus version of the Gospel, some fast-food religion, without any deep transformation of the self; and the result has been the spiritual disaster of "Christian" countries that tend to be as consumer-oriented, proud, warlike, racist, class conscious, and addictive as everybody else—and often more so, I'm afraid.[4]

These are strong words, but they tell an important truth and point to a dilemma the modern church faces and many of you have bumped up against—*we want things to be different but are often not willing to practice it in our own lives and experience.*

Prior to planting The Refuge in 2006, I spent years trying to encourage leadership in the churches we were part of to be open to the possibility of healing and recovery, not as a side ministry but embedded into the fabric of our community's life. With countless leaders and congregants I heard the same responses over and over: "We're not like those people." "I'm not an addict." "I just need Jesus." "I don't want to become too internally focused." Fear of intentional inner work is a large barrier for a lot of people and systems. I think some of this fear stems from our human tendency to avoid pain at all costs. Many of us were also taught that Jesus saves us from our pain and we're supposed to be "above it" instead of remembering Jesus entered pain directly—his own and the world's—to transform it. We can't convince others of their need for healing; we can only work on our own selves. Usually, as we are changed, the groups we are part of slowly begin to change also.

I hope each of you will be part of this kind of change. What happens at the micro-level affects the macro-level. The practice of healing isn't just for individuals, it's for groups and systems as well. Even though I often say, "I think the church needs a recovery meeting," I always add, "If the church won't go, we still can."

Wounded Healers

A few years ago I had the privilege of speaking at a Methodist seminary for their Addiction and Recovery Week; the conversations were rich and the hunger for healing inspiring. Even though I heard numerous stories from ministry leaders about the uphill battle of integrating anything related to the Twelve Steps and recovery into the wider body, I saw their determination to continue their own personal work despite the cost. Being in a room of wounded healers was profoundly encouraging.

Henri Nouwen—a Catholic priest who intimately knew pain, struggle, and doubt and one of the most prolific writers on spiritual healing—coined the term "wounded healer" in his compelling book *The Wounded Healer: Ministry in Contemporary Society*. He speaks of the importance of owning our unique story and wounds as our greatest strength to contribute to others:

> Nobody escapes being wounded. We are all wounded people, whether physically, emotionally, mentally, or spiritually. The main question is not, "How can we hide our wounds?" so we don't have to be embarrassed, but "How can we put our woundedness in the service of others?" When our wounds cease to be a source of shame, and become a source of healing, we have become wounded healers.[5]

The world is in desperate need of wounded healers.

We need more vulnerable, honest, humble men and women across ages and experiences who know they can't swoop in and save the day but are willing to engage in the marvelous work of healing presence with others. Practicing presence is essential in the practice of healing, and it's what wounded healers do best. Wounded healers know they can't change people through words, spiritual platitudes, or quick fixes. They know that sitting with people in the dark seems to make the most difference. In a culture that thrives on loud and fast, this simple act of presence breaks all the rules but turns out to be what people crave most. I can't count the number of times hurting people have shared that what healed them the most was experiencing "Jesus with skin on," flesh and blood human beings who were willing to hold their hand, listen to their brutal and beautiful stories, and offer compassion that didn't need words.

Through our son's death, *wounded healer* has taken on new meaning. No words can take away our pain. People who held us in the dark and kept us alive the first days when we weren't sure we could take our next breath knew the art of silence and presence . . . that the gaping wound of our hearts just needed to bleed. The thirteenth-century Sufi poet Rumi always has the simplest of truths: "The wound is the place where the Light enters you."

Like all of these transformational practices (and wild ways of Jesus), the practice of healing is not something we ever master. I have been intentionally working on my personal healing for well over two decades and some days it seems I have barely scratched the surface. The reason I'm still practicing healing is I have tasted the fruit of healing in my marriage, friendships, children, and with myself; I have grown exponentially since I first chose to be more honest and vulnerable, but there's always more. Healing starts with us. We must work on loving ourselves as a catalyst for loving others, acknowledging our tendency to want to help others instead of doing the much more vulnerable task of our own personal work. Healing can also come as we commit ourselves to an honest, reflective process in the stream of what is found in the Twelve Steps and the Beatitudes. These kinds of transformational principles aren't just for addicts. They're for all of us. Lastly, the practice of healing includes presence, offering ourselves as wounded healers in a world filled with people who feel alone in their struggle and need to know they're not.

Another way we can continue to practice healing individually, and also in our groups and systems, is to cultivate the practice of listening. There's a lot to learn when we offer more ears, less mouth in a world that thrives on loudness and division. That's the verb and practice we'll engage with next.

A PRAYER FOR HEALING

God, you are our healer, binding up wounds and making us whole.
Help us grow into your image as people of practice.
Give us courage to be honest.
Show us a better way.
Use our wounds to heal others.
Amen.

FOR PERSONAL REFLECTION

1. Consider your own journey of healing. What has it looked like for you? What were some of the obstacles you have faced along the way? What do you want to celebrate today?

2. How have you hidden some of the truth of your story from others to maintain a safe and comfortable distance from them? What has that created inside of you? How has it affected your relationships with others?
3. Consider what you checked on the unhealthy relationship patterns. What are some areas you know you need to keep working on in your healing process?
4. Take time to celebrate movement on the list of better practices. Remember where you've been and how far you've come. You can use this prompt: *Before, I didn't* _____, *but now I can do / am learning to* _____.
5. Who is a wounded healer in your life? How can you be one for others?

FOR GROUP DISCUSSION

1. What are some other words for *healing?* Make a list together.
2. Reflect on this statement: "One of the reasons the world is so screwed up right now is that we are, indeed, loving our neighbors as ourselves. The problem is that a lot of us actually hate ourselves." What resonates?
3. Read through the list of unhealthy patterns in a relationship. Risk making yourself vulnerable and share (to the level you feel comfortable sharing) some of the boxes you checked. How does it feel to say them out loud?
4. Likewise, share the checks and circles on the healthier relationship patterns—movement you want to celebrate and areas you want to keep working on.

5. What is your personal experience with the Twelve Steps and the Beatitudes as a pathway for healing?
6. How can you use your woundedness to be a healing presence for others individually? Corporately as a group?

TO PRACTICE

1. If you've never been, go to a Twelve Step, recovery, or support group and listen to the stories. Notice what resonates when you hear others share honestly and freely.
2. With a trusted safe friend, make time to honestly share some of the things you are currently struggling with in your life or some unhealthy patterns you are trying to break. What does it feel like to make space for this?
3. Consider who might be a wounded healer in your life; who has influenced your formation through their honesty and vulnerability? Tell them what they mean to you and what you've learned from them.
4. When someone asks you how you are doing and you're tempted to respond quickly with "Fine," try to be more honest. "I'm actually feeling _____." It's a simple practice but really challenging to do, and it's good to prepare yourself for some interesting reactions to your honesty!
5. Ask for help. Yes, do it! Take note of how it feels and what you learn from the experience.

DIG DEEPER

Breathing Under Water: Spirituality and the Twelve Steps by Richard Rohr

Codependent No More: How to Stop Controlling Others and Start Caring for Yourself by Melody Beattie

Daring Greatly: How the Courage to Be Vulnerable Transforms the Way We Live, Love, Parent, and Lead by Brené Brown

When Things Fall Apart: Heart Advice for Difficult Times by Pema Chödrön

CHAPTER 2

THE PRACTICE OF LISTENING

Lis·ten — ˈlis(ə)n
Verb / present participle: **listening**
1. To offer deliberate attention to what another person is expressing (verbal and nonverbal)
2. To receive input and information through conversation
3. To connect to the words of another and take action accordingly

> *Listen with the heart, and not just the ear.*[1]
> —Lonni Collins Pratt

A few years ago, The Refuge had the privilege of hosting Mark Charles, a Navajo American speaker, writer, and recent U.S. presidential candidate running as an independent. Mark is passionately dedicated to calling out the realities of church and U.S. history and the way it has ravaged his people. As we were intently listening and getting our souls rocked, I knew there were some in the room who were doing what we often do when we are uncomfortable with what we're hearing: we begin editing in our minds, "But what about . . ." or "Are you sure about that?" or "I think there are two sides to this story." No one said it out loud in that moment, but afterward that response emerged in several short conversations. I have empathy because I felt it too. As a white woman of privilege, no matter how dedicated I am to social justice issues, I retain a tendency toward denial. Editing what we hear and finding a way to chip away at it is a way we protect ourselves from pain and distance ourselves from others. We sometimes can't believe we are truly the kind of people who could commit such atrocities against others. We don't want to be held accountable for the sins of our ancestors and certainly don't want to believe we are still complicit in it today.

In short, we often don't want to listen.

In the same vein as the practice of healing, listening is one of the most underutilized practices today in the wider world, and even more often in the church. Yes, we are socialized to listen to pastors preach from the pulpit on Sunday, to read certain books by particular authors, or maybe occasionally hear a story from someone not like us. But to truly listen, to deeply engage in hearing another's perspective, experience, and story for deeper understanding and change—especially when it doesn't resonate with our perspective, experience, and story—is no easy task. We can hear someone's words and not actually listen. How often have you pretended like you were listening when you were actually just thinking about what you were going to say next? Or sat nodding, taking in information, knowing that you were never going to do anything with what you just heard? That's hearing, not listening.

Listening is about understanding. The founder of the International Listening Association, Ralph Nichols, reminds us, "The most basic of all human needs is the need to understand and be understood. The best way to understand people is to listen to them."[2] Like all of the practices in this book, none come without intention. They won't

drop out of the sky. We won't be able to check them off
our to-do list as something we've easily mastered or figured out a way to conquer. Rather, they are a way of being,
a way of moving in the world, a way of living out our faith
in a culture that is expecting us to show up in ways we are
known for—talking (usually loudly) instead of listening.
Author and spiritual philosopher Mark Nepo recognizes
the challenges of listening well:

> We must honor that listening is a personal pilgrimage
> that takes time and a willingness to circle back. With
> each trouble that stalls us and each wonder that lifts
> us, we are asked to put down our conclusions and
> feel and think anew. Unpredictable as life itself, the
> practice of listening is one of the most mysterious,
> luminous, and challenging art forms on Earth.[3]

Unfortunately, Christians have one of the worst reputations in the listening department—for good reason. As a
wider group, we often insulate ourselves from perspectives
that don't align with our experience or the homogeneity
to which we have become accustomed. Shared beliefs and
perspectives mark many of our communities, so having
a dissonant angle inserted can rattle and rock us. When
we're rattled and rocked, what do humans most naturally
do? Push back and protect. Say the word "white privilege"
today in certain circles and it's almost guaranteed there
will be particularly defensive responses. "I am sick of being
told I'm privileged," or "I am tired of being discriminated
against for being white," or "I worked hard to get where I
am in life" come to mind as commonly used first responses.

Social media confirms this data. Almost universally,
when I see friends' posts about racism in our country and
look briefly at the comments, practically every single thread
includes one of these three specific statements. My third
child, who is in his early twenties, led a diversity initiative at
his college, a historically white male institution connected

to the military. As a Hispanic young adult, Jamison found that fostering a spirit of listening to marginalized voices has been an uphill battle. Each time they began the conversations about race and inclusivity, the first responses were exactly these, often from the most churched and faithful. It's fascinating and deeply troubling.

The growing political divide and effects of relentless social media, along with theological splits carving our denominations and churches up on a daily basis, have increased the need to listen to each other while making it more challenging by the day. The intensity of perspectives, the heel-digging, and fear of the other is picking up speed. Some days it is not only exhausting but also terrifying. We wonder: *Will we ever be able to find our way back to each other? Can we heal the deep divides between us? Is it possible to break down the walls that separate our differences and find common ground?*

We have a lot of work to do to become better listeners as followers of Jesus, but I have great hope for change and transformation through applying better skills to the process and practicing them. But remember, even with the best guidance, we will stumble and bumble along the way; we will sometimes fail miserably and other times make great strides. The catalyst that will compel us is the desire to become better listeners in a world that finds them rare.

More Ears, Less Mouth

At The Refuge, we have a bimonthly group called Advocates Learning Lab that is dedicated to skills, support, and sustainability for people who journey with others in hard places. It is one of the spaces I most value in our community because it exposes me to a wide variety of perspectives and practical tools not only as an advocate but also as a pastor, parent, and friend. Every year we add to our "Advocates Toolbox," a document filled with our best practices. Because we're always learning, we like to update it with fresh insights, questions, and possibilities.

One of the toolbox sections is called "Important Things Advocates Need to Remember." My dear friend, a recovering cocaine addict, stellar listener, and advocate for people in hard places, shared this little gem: *We need more ears, less mouth*. More ears, less mouth. There is no question that to listen more and talk less is one of the most important things an advocate—and all of us developing the practice of listening—can remember.

More ears, less mouth is a simple practice but is extremely tricky to live out. We are so accustomed to talking, to finding ways to insert our opinion, thought, perspective, or kernel of wisdom, and make sure we are heard, that we miss out on truly hearing others. I was recently with my friend Cole, who struggles with some mental and emotional challenges. In his mid-twenties and constantly bullied as a kid, words are not the easiest for him; however, when they do flow out, we all try to stop and listen. Even though I am pretty good at listening in the moment, I often feel an urge to add a little extra Kathy wisdom to the mix, to offer a word of encouragement, to try to explain something more clearly to supposedly help relieve his anxiety (as in, my anxiety). Yeah, you guessed it—not helpful. More ears, less mouth are what he usually always needs the most.

He's been growing in courage and health and recently told me, "Kathy, that's not what I need right now. I just need to say it out loud and be heard." I was so proud of him! Then I was angry with myself because I am the one who teaches this stuff and should obviously know better! However, I'm human too. As we practice we must remember we are all learning together and are sure to make countless mistakes. The question is what I will do with feedback—will I use it to change or keep doing what feels easiest for me in the moment? That's a question for all of us. I will also add that this kind of feedback Cole shared with me came from years of relationship. My guess is many others we have engaged with over time feel exactly like

Cole and don't say it to us out of fear—or assuming that again, we won't really listen.

The simple practice of more ears, less mouth is worth trying to integrate into our lives and experience. Try it and see what happens.

Dignified Dialogue

While more ears and less mouth is the best starting place to listening, we also need to develop the ability to engage in harder conversations and heal deep divisions through healthy dialogue. Years ago I served on the advisory team of the Denver Faith and Justice Conference and was tasked with developing guidelines for difficult conversations related to specific social justice issues. Participants in this gathering hold a wide range of theological differences, ranging from more conservative evangelical to strongly progressive. We could feel the divide widening between these groups and wanted to find a way to foster robust conversations about tough topics with solid guidelines. It was a fun project. With input from some of the other advisory team members, we settled on these "Five Principles of Dignified Dialogue" as simple guides for holding space across differences in conversations:

1. Remember that each person is first and foremost a child of God, created in God's image, worthy of dignity and respect.
2. Ask questions to clarify understanding instead of only making statements.
3. Stick with "I think" or "My opinion is" or "My interpretation is" instead of making generalizations like "God says" or "God thinks" or "The Bible says."
4. Remember that this is an opportunity to listen and learn, not convince, give advice, or change anyone else.
5. Honor the time with brevity and give others a chance to finish their thoughts before sharing yours.

Over the years, Dignified Dialogue has been integrated into different venues and experiences in our city and beyond because we experienced firsthand what can happen with a simple but meaningful framework to guide us. We read these principles at the beginning of gatherings not as a be-all and end-all but as a lens to consider as we strengthen our listening skills and hold space for each other.

Because the list sounds so elementary, it can be easy to say, "Yeah, yeah, I know these. I've got it" and quickly skip over their wisdom and value without engaging with how difficult it is to live them out practically. I'm going to briefly walk through each of them to add flesh to their bones. As I do, consider conversations or groups where these weren't applied. *What ended up happening? How did you show up in the group? What happened with the power dynamics within the conversation? What was the outcome?* Think, too, of moments where some of these principles were utilized and you experienced something different, better, healthier. *What did you observe in group members? How did the overall feel of the conversation shift?*

1. The Best Starting Place. Starting with the divine image of God embedded in each and every human being is central to listening. When people differ from us, especially politically or theologically, we easily default to believing we are better or more superior than them. It's not always conscious, but entering into conversation with a one-up or one-down mentality is one of the biggest misses in the practice of listening. Social media has made this much worse, creating deep divisions on who's right, who's wrong, who's less, and who's more. Realizing we are equal as God's children, made in God's image, and worthy of dignity and respect is the most essential starting place. During the 2012 presidential election, I saw a meme that I still remember. It was of Democratic President Barack Obama and Republican nominee Mitt Romney and said "Made in the image of God" twice with arrows pointing to each of them. No matter how you may have voted, yes, they both sure are.

Every person we are in relationship with—no matter how different, difficult, or completely exasperating they are or how foreign to our culture or experience—is, indeed, made in the image of God and worthy of dignity and respect.

2. Questions Are Always Better. Next, I would much rather make statements than ask questions. I love to get my two cents in, to pontificate my opinion, to find an opening in a conversation and slip in my perspective to make sure they know where I'm coming from. Don't you feel that way sometimes? Not all relate to this impulse, but for those who do, an excellent way to strengthen our skills as listeners is to practice asking questions instead of making statements. You will quickly see how hard it is. I am steeped in this work and know better, and I still leave some interesting conversations realizing that I worked to sneak in my statements instead of asking questions to learn more from the other person. Parker Palmer, a Quaker and one of my favorite wisdom teachers, says, "Honest, open questions are countercultural."[4]

I wholeheartedly agree.

3. Don't Throw Down the God Card. Number three—sticking with "I think" or "My opinion is" or "My interpretation is" instead of "God says" or "The Bible says"—is especially difficult for Christians who feel the weight of the important task of speaking truth to others. Many of us come from faith traditions that fostered a culture of "we need to tell others what Scripture says," so this is a challenging habit to break. Over the past decade my faith has significantly shifted. With it is a new recognition of the vast possibilities for Scripture interpretation. There are many ways to live out our faith, and none of us have the market cornered on it. Some of you are cheering right now while others of you feel that uncomfortable kink that rises up when hearing things contrary to your beliefs. You might want to say, "But what about . . ." or interject, "Scripture says . . ."—I hear you! Yet, until we begin to let go of sharing these clauses with others, we won't ever truly listen.

We need to own that anything we share is only our particular interpretation of a Scripture, perspective, or value. This is why using "I think" or "My opinion is" or "My interpretation is" is incredibly freeing—and compelling in relationship. We can still share freely in conversation what we think or believe, but we stop playing the God card or Bible card unfairly.

4. Please, No Unsolicited Advice. One of my favorite principles in Twelve Step recovery meetings is that we never give advice, fix, or spout Scripture to others. When people share their experience, strength, and hope, we usually end with "Thank you for sharing" and let things be. We resist our urge to make things better, tip things in a direction we feel more comfortable with, or share our words of wisdom, thinking it will make a significant impact in the moment. In Dignified Dialogue, it's similar. If we make another person's sharing about our wisdom, advice, or own suffering, it immediately shuts down listening. Recently, I was in a group of pastors from around the United States who were dreaming of future churches. We didn't have guidelines for the group discussion, and it was fascinating to watch how much unsolicited advice was tossed around freely: "Have you tried . . . ? Have you read . . . ? Here's what helps me . . ."

In difficult conversations about race, sexuality, and theological differences, where listening and learning is paramount, we need to practice the discipline of holding back from convincing anyone of anything in that moment. I always say, *"No one is one sentence away from changing their lives or minds completely."* Yet we often operate in conversations like that, thinking, "If I just show them this fact or share this piece of information or perspective, it will change everything."

It won't.

5. Shorter Helps. Last, the practice of brevity in sharing helps in these tricky conversations. We all have probably experienced that sinking feeling in a group where someone starts rambling nonstop without taking a breath or pause, with no concept of how much time they've chewed up. Remember, more ears, less mouth? However, I want to clarify that I'm talking about those whose dominant voices are most often heard. This principle is not to minimize voices from the margins. If your voice has been marginalized, please know this: *We need more spaces and places where your voice is magnified, amplified, and valued while those with power and privilege practice better listening.*

My hope isn't that you isolate Dignified Dialogue principles to only difficult or scheduled conversations. All five of them are good for most any situation where we're trying to practice listening.

Stories Change Everything

One of the most central pieces of listening is to honor and hold each other's real stories. Stories change everything. When we know a person's story, we have a connection that is completely different than hearing about a concept or idea. Hearing about illegal immigration as a political sound bite is radically different than being in relationship with our neighbor who is raising a U.S.-born child, working three jobs, and living in constant fear. Conversations about LGBTQ+ realities go an entirely new direction when we are holding a child, sibling, or dear friend we love and live alongside in the forefront of our minds and hearts. Abortion debates take on new meaning when we know the real story of someone who was faced with that difficult dilemma and chose one. Listening includes empathy—the ability to understand and share the feeling of another.

When I first began telling my story about a past abortion over two decades ago, I was completely floored by how many people either had the same experience or could identify with the shame and pain I experienced and how hard it was to talk about in church. Stories do change everything, and this is why we need to cultivate the practice of listening to them better instead of relying on removed-from-our-heart concepts. Parker Palmer reminds us,

> Instead of telling our valuable stories, we seek safety in abstractions, speaking to each other about our opinions, ideas, and beliefs rather than about our lives. Academic culture [and I would add contemporary Christian culture] blesses this practice by insisting that the more abstract our speech, the more likely we are to touch the universal truths that unite us. But what happens is exactly the reverse: as our discourse becomes more abstract, the less connected we feel. There is less sense of community among intellectuals than in the most "primitive" society of storytellers.[5]

Stories create community. Sometimes we need a little help to learn how to draw others' stories out through the practice of listening.

After we practiced Dignified Dialogue in a few venues, a local nonprofit leader who has committed his life to bridging the divides between our differences, asked me how we could take the conversations to a deeper level over time. It is true, while Dignified Dialogue principles are an excellent start for cultivating better spaces for healthier listening, we also need skills for ongoing dialogue that moves listening into deeper understanding. In response, I created a list of possible questions called "Deeper Dignified Dialogue" that can help us engage more deeply in listening to each other, especially across vast socioeconomic, racial, gender, theological, and political differences. This book is about developing more tangible tools to live out our faith through courageous practice, and this list is something to add to your toolbox.

Deeper Dignified Dialogue

Some questions to cultivate deeper conversations together:

— Tell me more about your story of your family, work, and what you're most passionate about.
— What are some of the primary things that influenced you to believe what you now believe?
— How have some of your views changed over time?
— What troubles you about where you have currently landed? What doubts do you have about your position or perspective?
— What brings you the most peace? What parts feel most clear?
— How have you wrestled with the Scriptures about this?
— What do you fear? How has fear influenced you?
— What misperceptions do you think people might have about you or your views?
— What have been some of the costs to your beliefs (relationships, church, jobs, etc.)?
— How have you felt misunderstood?
— What are ways I might be able to help you feel more understood? (Bonus points for this one!)
— What helps you hear stories better? How have others engaged with yours in a meaningful way?

I hope you will add some of your own questions to this list. Hopefully, we're all continually adding tools over time, not as trite questions to pull out mechanically but as helpful ideas to integrate in our own contexts as people of practice.

Whose Voices Aren't Being Heard?

As a female pastor with evangelical roots, I have been in many rooms where I am one of the only women in a sea of men. I have seen positive shifts over the past few years but the grooves of patriarchy are deep, and we have a long way to go. The dominant voices in many of our groups and systems remain held by white males. I recently saw a picture of a large, international, denominational strategic meeting focused on the future of the church, and 100 percent of the people present around the table were white men. One hundred percent! In this current climate, with our entire country focused on the importance of increasing diversity, it saddened me but didn't shock me, either. It's a reminder that despite the strides we're making, many of our systems are completely insulated from the margins. When people live inside these kinds of protected bubbles, we become isolated from hearing different voices and disconnected from real stories of people not like us.

These days, with the acceleration of Black Lives Matter, #MeToo, and other strong social justice movements, many dominant groups are recognizing the need to listen to voices we haven't heard before. I am glad for this, but remember: hearing and listening are not the same thing. Hearing is paying attention to words that are shared. Listening is about being open to being taught and transformed by what we hear.

To develop the skill of listening we can ask ourselves a few core questions, both personally and in the groups we are part of: *Whose voices aren't being heard? Who have I not been taught by? Whose voice is missing in this conversation?* Every group is different, but most are probably lacking at least one particular voice, no matter how intent on diversity it is. I have been part of a wonderful, inclusive, and humble interfaith clergy group for five years, and to this day there has never been a Native American representative at the table. I love this group of leaders and its call to bring together representatives across every faith; a beautiful mix of different strains of Christian, Jewish, Muslim, Hindu, Buddhist, Baha'i, Unitarian Universalist, Mormon, Roman Catholic, and Religious Science, it is quite diverse. Yet, we are missing one of the most robust and rich traditions in our history by not having a Native voice at the table. I hope to be part of changing that, but it points to the question we need to keep asking: *Whose voice is missing?*

A few months ago, my friend Chuck facilitated our House of Refuge, an eclectic group of men and women across ages and experiences who come together at our house each week for a potluck dinner and spiritual conversation. We call it "spiritual show and tell," and whoever facilitates can bring whatever they are learning or wrestling with or wondering about to the group. That particular night, Chuck, a millennial dad of two young girls, a husband who loves *Star Wars* and cooking and gives me hope for the future, set us up with a raw, powerful reflection about how sick he was about patriarchy. He then asked one simple question: "Women, what do men need to hear about the realities of patriarchy?" He asked the men not to speak for the entire night but to solely listen. Whoa, was it powerful, hearing the real stories that barely scratched the surface, and what it felt like to have that space. Women spoke about things they had never had a platform to bring up before. Over the years, I have shared my experiences with patriarchy in a lot of venues, but each time it's been fairly orchestrated and calculated. This simple, pure, unexpected, and much-needed opportunity made me wish more people would create such opportunities. Will you? Whose voices aren't being heard, and how can you listen to them?

While listening through in-the-flesh relationship with eyes, ears, and hearts in the mix is always best, there's also room to expand what we're listening to in other ways. *What books are we reading? What podcasts are we listening to? What sermons are we reflecting on?* If they all tend to be the same strain of thinking or from the same gender or color, it's time to develop a wider repertoire and add more diversity of thought and experience to our listening. We probably won't be quite as comfortable or feel the same level of inspiration that comes when we rely on teachers who look like us, think like us, believe like us. But we will grow because of it. I recently had a painful moment of self-awareness and discovered that while I try to keep up on many social justice issues, most all the teachers I was listening to outside of The Refuge community were white, educated men and women. I've been trying to add people of color and leaders from the margins and my world keeps expanding, but I've got a long way to go.

As we transition to our next practice of loving, remember that the practice of listening isn't only centered on social justice issues. Listening is a core practice that infiltrates all our relationships and starts with our own self-awareness at how hard it is to do. It's about more ears, less mouth. It's listening to real stories that change everything. It's about empathy. It's about letting go of control and letting others teach us. It's making room for new voices at the table.

Imagine how different the world could be if excellent listeners permeated our families, neighborhoods, workplaces, churches, and organizations? As we practice better listening in these smaller conversations, we're making inroads to shift the larger ones too. This is why we need to keep bravely practicing together.

Building on the foundations of healing and listening, the next practice we're going to wrestle with together is also a cornerstone to transformation—the practice of loving. Love definitely can't be mastered. We'll spend our entire lifetimes being challenged to love, but that's what a life of practice is all about.

A PRAYER FOR LISTENING

God, you are the great listener, holding our stories and listening to
the cries of our heart.
Help us grow into your image as people of practice.
May we learn how to hold space to better listen.
Honor differences.
Seek out missing voices.
Make room at the table.
Be humbled by stories.
Transformed by what we learn.
Amen.

FOR PERSONAL REFLECTION

1. What are some relationships in which you feel truly listened to? What do they do or say that helps you feel heard?
2. How do you identify with *"more ears, less mouth"*? Think of a relationship where you know you need to practice this.
3. Reflect personally on the Five Principles of Dignified Dialogue. Consider how some of these guidelines could improve a conversation you're currently having or a difficult relationship. What could you possibly do differently? Is there a way you can apply any of these skills to help strengthen it?
4. Who are some missing voices in your repertoire of teachers? Who do you need to consider adding to the mix?

FOR GROUP DISCUSSION

1. What are ways you are trying to cultivate the practice of listening in some of your current relationships? Share some personal examples with the group.
2. Consider the Five Principles of Dignified Dialogue. Which come the easiest for you? Which are the most difficult?
3. What other questions would you add to the list of Deeper Dignified Dialogue questions to more deeply engage with others?   1, 3
4. If you are a white male, your group has held most of the words in many contexts throughout history. What does this chapter on listening challenge you to consider?
5. If you are a straight, white person, male or female, what voices do you know you need to listen to more intentionally?
6. If you are someone whose voice has been marginalized, what helps you feel more heard and understood?
7. Make a list together of voices and teachers that have inspired and challenged you for other group members to consider.

TO PRACTICE

1. Give more ears, less mouth a try in a conversation. What happened when you talked less and listened more?
2. Consider a conversation you are dreading about political or theological differences. Before the next time you get together, review the principles of

Dignified Dialogue and try to apply some of them. What happened?

3. Ask more questions and make fewer statements.

4. Walk through some of the questions for Deeper Dignified Dialogue and glean a few that you can use in a conversation. How did it help you discover more of that person's story?

5. If you are in leadership, have a conversation with your team about whose voices are missing. What are some ways you might be able to make room at the table for them?

6. Add some new authors that you normally wouldn't listen to—to your reading list, blog or social media feed, or podcast list.

7. Consider creating a space for your group where you give the floor to marginalized voices with no other comments, just listening.

DIG DEEPER

Difficult Conversations: How to Discuss What Matters Most by Douglas Stone, Bruce Patton, and Sheela Heen

Healing the Heart of Democracy: The Courage to Create a Politics Worthy of the Human Spirit by Parker Palmer

Nonviolent Communication: A Language of Life by Marshall Rosenberg

Radical Hospitality: Benedict's Way of Love by Lonni Collins Pratt

CHAPTER 3

THE PRACTICE
OF LOVING

Love—*luhv*
Verb / present participle: **loving**
1. To feel fondness for and vulnerability with another person
2. To show tangible care and compassion
3. To express feelings of connection, value, and respect

Love is the way messengers from the mystery tell us things.
Love is the mother. We are her children. She shines inside us,
Visible-invisible, as we trust or lose trust,
Or feel it start to grow again.

—Rumi[1]

The word "love" gets tossed around a lot, not only in Christian circles but across faiths and among secular groups as well. *We just need to love one another. All you need is love. What the world needs now is love, sweet love. Love your neighbor. Put love into the world. Love wins. Choose love not hate.*

I love the word *love*! More love is greatly needed in a world filled with billions of disconnected and fragmented humans. Love heals. Love binds us together. Love helps us become healthier human beings. However, for as much as we talk about love, preach about love, and tell people they should love, we often aren't that great at practicing it.

As I highlighted in chapter 1, "The Practice of Healing," one of the most quoted Scriptures is Jesus' command that we love God and love our neighbors as ourselves. This wasn't new material; Jesus drew directly from the Hebrew Scriptures, which is why love is one of Judaism's highest values as well. *Love God, love people* is an extremely popular Christian church slogan for a reason. It simplifies what we often make complicated with dogma, doctrine, and denominations when for the most part people really do want to live a life of loving God and people. However, Christians and Jews don't have the market cornered on the commandment to love; all the major world religions place love at the center of most of their practices, each with different languages and perspectives.

In Buddhism, there are four kinds of love: loving-kindness, compassion, appreciative joy, and equanimity. The Baha'i faith focuses on love that flows from God to human beings, from human beings to God, the love we have for ourselves, and the love human beings have for one another. A core framework of Hinduism is dharma, which centers on duty, virtue, morality; to love is people's service to others and God. In Islam, the practice of loving through tangible help for the poor and needy is central. Many atheists I know are more deeply dedicated to loving others than those who profess faith. Love is not limited by a particular religion. It's a universal language expressed in many different ways.

While *love* often easily slips off the tip of the tongue in conversations and dreams about how the world should be, we also know that we are often the worst representations of loving. A few years ago I conducted an experiment on my Facebook page, asking friends to share what they think of when they hear the word "Christian." Words poured in, threaded with a profoundly common theme—*judgmental, mean, critical, cliquey, and exclusive*—just to name a few. When I next asked, "When you think of 'Jesus,' what comes to mind?" Their answers were what we might expect—*love, compassion, mercy, grace, forgiveness, peace.*

Gandhi is often falsely attributed with the famous quote, "I like your Christ. I do not like your Christians. Your Christians are so unlike your Christ." There's actually no record of him saying it directly, but most of us can identify with the meaning underneath. Jesus embodied love—sacrificial, uncomfortable, messy love—and called us to it as followers of his way. Yet, Christians are often not reflections of Christ and are far more known for our desire for comfort, separation from the world, and exclusion.

I used to be proud to have the title "Christian," making sure that others knew I was part of that team. Now, as several decades have passed and I have witnessed far too many discrepancies between words and actions, sometimes I cringe when people ask me. Do you know this feeling, when you're on an airplane or in a line talking to a stranger and somehow the question comes up in the conversation: "Are you a Christian?" My response has now become, "Well, um, it depends on what you mean by Christian."

However, while it is true that the world has been exposing some of the hypocrisies of the Christian faith, I also see an upsurge of people desiring to live out a life of love in tangible ways. It feels like a groundswell of desire to be legitimate practitioners of love. It's probably why you picked up this book. You've experienced the disconnect between what we say and what we do. Some of us have been damaged by phrases like "love the sinner, hate the sin" or know others who have. Others of us know our time on earth is limited and don't want to spend it just *talking about* love. We want to *actually* love. We want to be tangible reflections of love in the world.

Corrective Experiences

There's a term in therapy I resonate deeply with called *corrective experiences*. Essentially, it's an experience that repairs the traumatic influence of previous experiences — *an encounter that somehow heals, repairs, or shifts a previous trauma, assumption, or wound.*

Most people in the world have a lot of pain related to life and faith. We've been used, abused, hurt, cast aside. Others have been undervalued, ignored, dismissed. Some of us have specific experiences we remember vividly; others are a blur of a lifetime of hard things strung together that create a pervasive negative feeling that we live with day to day. Some of the most prominent pain people share often seems to boil down to feeling unloved, not enough, unworthy, alone, and unprotected.

I believe in every part of my soul that one of the most world-changing practices of love is to help create corrective experiences for people — to have them experience, in the flesh, something different than the damage they received in their family, life, or church.

Instead of passing judgment, we love unconditionally. Instead of subtly or directly expecting people to change on our terms, we can accept them as they are. Instead of cementing the message that certain people don't belong, we can welcome everyone freely to the table. Instead of shutting down someone's painful story, we can listen and resist our urge to fix. Instead of expecting people to believe what I do, I can honor their theologies and trust God is at work in their lives as much as God is at work in mine. Instead of seeing ourselves different from people, we can notice what we have in common.

This is love.

This is being generous with our lives.

This is what will heal wounds and help crack open a door that has been slammed shut out of pain.

I have been journeying with LGBTQ+ friends for over two decades now and many of the stories are the same. When they came out to families or church, honoring their true identities in the light, most were met with what they expected—shame, disapproval, withdrawal of love. Their deepest fears came true, cementing the damaging messages even more firmly.

My friend Amy Jo was raised in a staunchly conservative evangelical family, and when she landed on the truth that she was lesbian she knew it was going to cause a deep rift in relationship with them. She was in the middle of a radical faith shift where, on top of it all, she didn't know what she believed about God either and was hesitant to tell her truth out of fear. However, she started with The Refuge family first, sharing honestly and freely with a small group of us to start, and then our wider community over time. We offered what her family couldn't—unconditional love and acceptance in the moment. It didn't matter what she believed or didn't believe or whether she was gay or straight. We loved her for her and would stand by her no matter what.

She had a corrective experience.

Sure, the longing for her family's acceptance didn't automatically disappear, but Amy Jo had something to hold onto that was real, tangible, and rooted. She said it this way, "I learned through my Refuge friends that my sexual identity made no difference in my lovability, value, or validity as a person of faith. They literally saved my life." Corrective experiences can do that.

A lot of people are done with words. They don't want to hear the word *love* tossed around but then experience something completely different. Amy Jo didn't need to hear, "We love you but not your sin" or "You just need to . . ." or "We'll pray for you." She needed to have a tangible corrective experience, one totally different from what she had experienced in her family and prior faith systems.

She needed to experience love and acceptance over the long haul, not as a special project but as an equal, valuable human being, made in the image of God, worthy of dignity and respect.

This is where we have such a beautiful and meaningful role to play as individuals and communities longing to change the landscape of our current culture. It's also why I am so deeply dedicated to creating spaces and places where people can practice these ways of moving in the world that heal, transform, and redeem.

It also makes me think of Richard Rohr's words: "The best criticism of the bad is the practice of the better."[2] It's often easier to get caught up in criticizing Christians and other people of faith for the harshness they've deposited into the world and spend my time complaining about them instead of loving. *The best criticism of the bad is the practice of the better.*" Ragging on others won't change the world, but creating corrective experiences for people in desperate need of them definitely will.

God First?

I live in a world where people are fairly cynical about all things God and church. Many used to be faithful followers of Jesus, deeply dedicated to their faith, so much so that often they sacrificed their own livelihood and care of their souls to believe and belong in a certain way. When I toss out words like *love God*, many people both in and outside of The Refuge community become a little allergic (is that you right now?), wondering if in order to play they have to believe a certain thing again. For me, the answer is clear—*No, you don't have to love God a particular way in order for the love you spread in the world to count.* However, I do believe this: Recognizing God's love for humans and the incredible beauty and creativity of creation helps ground and strengthen us. Henri Nouwen's book *Life of the Beloved: Spiritual Living in a Secular World* is one of my favorites because it reminds us: "Becoming the Beloved means letting the truth of our Belovedness become enfleshed in everything we think, say, or do."[3]

But we don't have to *love God a certain way* in order to love.

The bigger problem, I think, is that many Christians spend far more of their time and energy on the loving God part and forget the other two parts of the passage *loving our neighbor and loving ourselves.* Our theology and practice become centered on a vertical relationship with God where we espouse a theology of "It's just me and Jesus" or "God is enough" or "God and I are good; I don't need anyone else." I've heard this from folks countless times over the decades and believe it's a convenient way to protect ourselves from other forms of love. It's a religious defense mechanism that guards us against the bloody, messy, and vulnerable work of the second part of Jesus' summation of the greatest commandment. It also makes *going to church* far more important than *being the church.* In some ways, *loving God* is easier because it's more elusive and ethereal. Real humans, in-the-flesh, bugging, bothering, irritating, and angering us is a whole different story.

Also, it's important to highlight that a lot of us are experiencing a faith shift in which our images of God are radically changing, and we just can't connect with God in the same ways we used to. Loving God is not what we're feeling at the moment, but our desire to sort out our relationship with God is still strong. When we've grown up with a theology that depicts God as harsh, judgmental, behavior-centered, and prone to wrath, it's really difficult to feel loved or to want to love that kind of God. Sometimes, the most loving thing we can do is leave God as we once knew God and begin to reimagine the possibility of a more expansive, loving, and compassionate relationship. Even though faith deconstructing is often gravely misperceived by those who haven't experienced it, it is usually always catalyzed by the longing for more free, full, and expansive connection with God and others. On this one, I truly believe God would never say, "You've got to love me a certain way that others tell you is right before you can love others." Instead, I imagine God always whispering, "You're loved. You're loved. You're loved. Now pass it on."

Who Is Our Neighbor?

Many of us grew up watching *Mister Rogers' Neighborhood* on public television and can still sing the words we heard every episode—"Won't you be, won't you be, won't you be my neighbor?" Fred Rogers's focus was always on helping kids learn to be a good neighbor to others. Over and over, Jesus' teachings point in that direction also. In the story of the Good Samaritan in Luke 10, Jesus illuminates what we are called to do for our neighbors—stop, care, help, sacrifice—and how easy it is to just walk by and only take care of ourselves.

Who is our neighbor? Is it the person you live next to in your apartment or cul-de-sac? Is it your parents, your kids, your siblings? Is it your coworkers? People who live across the continent from you in a shack? I think of our neighbors as anyone in our lives that we live, love, and learn alongside. These folks can be in our most intimate relationships all the way out to groups of people we will never personally know. They are our fellow humans, people we inhabit this earth with who are made of flesh and blood and will return to dust in the end just as sure as we will.

Some will be up close and some will be far away, but no matter what, Jesus calls us to love.

Yet, it is also far easier to love people who think, believe, look like, and act like us, than it is to love neighbors who are vastly different. For many years my husband and I were in churches that were consistently filled with essentially the same kind of person—white, middle-class, fairly well-educated, mostly parents, and resourced financially, emotionally, and physically. We did a wonderful job of loving one another, but truly had no idea what it meant to love people not like us. Insulated from reality, in the words of an old friend, "we kept shining the light in our own eyes."

Thankfully, over time, as I began to tell my real story more honestly and connect with people in recovery, my world expanded. I sat next to men who lived outside, women who lived on disability checks and had never been to a baseball game, people of all ages, colors, faiths, life experiences, and more—all trying to get sober, to heal, grow, and change our lives. It opened up a whole new world, and now I could never go back. The texture and beauty of diversity cannot be measured and we can never find it if we keep remaining safely protected from our neighbors.

In the bubble I used to live in, relationships with people of other faiths were also considered taboo. Muslims, Jews, Unitarian Universalists, Hindus, Buddhists were seen as people who needed Jesus, and we either needed to convert them or be careful around them for fear of being deceived ourselves. There really weren't any other options. I am pretty sure that's not very neighborly. When I joined a multifaith clergy group in Denver a chunk of years ago, I received a true and transformational gift. When we sit at the wonderfully diverse table across faiths eating lunch together each month, we are not there to convince anyone of anything. We're there to listen. To learn. To love. To appreciate the beauty and wisdom of our neighbors of different faiths, to find what we have in common and celebrate that. To respect our diversity and be grateful we are all working for love and justice in different ways. That's it, nothing more. No hidden agendas, no secret motives to convert one another to our faiths.

Last spring, during the season of Ramadan for my Muslim friends, a new local imam shared about their core practice in their faith while people from eight other faith traditions asked thoughtful questions. Love was in that room. Mutual respect, a genuine desire to learn, and kindred friendship; that sure looks like love to me.

Brian McLaren, one of the wisest voices on a more generous orthodoxy and practice, offers this encouraging image:

> In my most hopeful moments, I imagine the Spirit of God calling Christians to a greater depth and breadth of aliveness . . . and at the same time, calling Muslims, Jews, Hindus, Buddhists, agnostics, and atheists to the same reality. So, just as the first words of Genesis describe the Spirit hovering over the primal waters, I dare to believe the life-giving Spirit hovers over the fluid elements of human culture, including religion. I wonder what might happen if we opened ourselves to the possibility that it isn't which religion or philosophy we belong to that counts as much as how we respond to that invitation of the Spirit.[4]

In a global world, the idea of neighbor also takes on new meaning. We're all connected in our shared humanity, but at the smallest level, the question for each of us is still the same: How can we love our neighbors more freely, more fully?

Including the Word "Love" Doesn't Mean It Is Loving

Sometimes we think we're being loving neighbors when we're really not. Years ago, before my faith radically shifted and I embraced a more inclusive and incarnational theology, I used this common phrase more than a few times: "Well, I love the sinner, but I hate the sin." Have you heard this one yourself? Have you said it — or are currently saying it — to others?

I have made my share of amends both in real life and in my heart over the years for the damage that this phrase—and theology—perpetuates. In a recent conversation with some folks, they used it so matter-of-factly, saying, "Well, we love the sinner but hate the sin. God is clear on that," and assuming I agreed. I felt my body tense, my heart clench. I responded kindly but passionately, "I hear you but do you understand that what you are saying to one of your closest friends is we can't love *YOU*?" I wanted to add a host of other things but stuck with this: "There are plenty of Christians who love the Bible and are faithful followers of Jesus and see the Scriptures differently from what you've been taught, and that phrase is a direct and deep violation of a person's identity. It is never, ever felt as loving. Ever."

I could feel a painful disconnect in the conversation, their desire to love but achieving the opposite effect. Our conversation ended with a strange mix of awkwardness and kindness, and I know their hearts are sincere. However, I'll hold to this: I've never yet met someone who felt loved by this phrase.

If you're reading and feel comfortable with "love the sinner, hate the sin," I'd encourage you to consider some of the excellent resources on the practice of including—available at the end of chapter 4—to unpack issues related to sexuality and faith and to hear more clearly from those who have been deeply wounded by it. For those of you reading this who have been harmed by this damaging form of love or been told that your support of your child, sibling, or close friend is a violation of God's law, I am so sorry. That is wrong. *You are loved just as you are, truly, madly, deeply.* For allies, your unconditional love for your friends or family member is something to be celebrated as a beautiful testament of the kind of love this world desperately needs to practice. We need to put a period after *love* in this sentence.

We love.

Period.

There's another phrase that, as we are growing in the practice of love, we may also want to reconsider. When talking about becoming more incarnational or missional people and communities, how many of you have heard someone say or said yourself, "I just want to 'love on _____' (fill in the blank with any kind of group—people who are homeless, single moms, struggling families, kids in need)?

How does this sound to you if you are the one on the underside of that love? This concept gets under my skin because it is infused with superiority, separateness, and pride. Who likes to be the one who's being *loved on*? Nobody I know! In fact, a lot of my friends on the margins can smell out people who want to *love on* them right away because it usually means that they are being viewed as a project. Loving others isn't about us doing what we think is right for someone else; that's called imposing our values and ideas onto other people. Loving others isn't about our need to feel like heroes and saving the day for someone else *on our terms*. Real love is about being with people.

The Refuge partners with a lot of community agencies in our local area. Many are very skeptical of Christians for good reason and the kind of trust and respect we have built over the years hasn't come from words. It's come from actions. They now see that when they call we aren't focused on "helping those poor people who need to be loved on and know Jesus." Rather, we are dedicated to embodying love, as best we can, through tangible presence, meeting practical needs, and offering unconditional acceptance. So many people are used to having agendas placed on them when it comes to love—*we'll love you more if you believe a certain way, act a particular way, do things the way we want you to do them.* On good days, I like to say that one of The Refuge's greatest gifts is that we are under-resourced with an extremely limited budget (on bad days I want to curl up in the fetal position and cry). However, it's easy to throw money at people in the name of love. Friendship, conversation, and presence can be totally and completely free. Yes, love is free.

Also, a lot of us can get overwhelmed by the needs. Everywhere we look there's someone to love and help, an organization to support, a GoFundMe to contribute to, a cause to get involved with where we can show our desire to love our neighbors with actions not just words. Feeling like our love has to be big to make a difference reminds me of a simple statement that some attribute to Mother Teresa: "If you can't feed 100 people, just feed one." I'll extrapolate from this principle. *If you can't love 100 people, just love one.*

If you can't love 100 people, just love one.

Don't get paralyzed by the need to love a certain way or formalize it or have it be legitimized by a certain ministry or program. Remember, simple, kind acts of love go further than we think, especially in a harsh and cruel world. Let us never underestimate what a tangible expression of love might mean for someone. What a cup of cold water might mean for another. The Refuge recently started a shower truck program, where people can get a free shower at our Refuge Café. This simple act of having an accessible place to get clean in a safe and comfortable environment has been transforming for folks trying to get on their feet in our community. Some weeks we have a bunch of people, other weeks we have just a few, and recently we had only one. His smile when he walked out made it all worth it.

One's always better than none.

Loving Others Is Often Easier
Than Loving Ourselves

As hard as it is to love our neighbors and people not like us, it's often even harder to love the person who is closest to us and knows us the best, the person we live and breathe and intersect with every waking moment of every day —*ourselves*.

Bad theology is at the core of some of this self-hatred, which we've already discussed in "The Practice of Healing." When you're taught you are a miserable wretch, and the theology of total depravity is embedded in your soul and experience, it's hard to untangle. I facilitate several groups online related to church woundedness and deconstructing faith. Core to each of these conversations is the damage that churches have imposed on people by telling them that they are nothing without God, that without Jesus God cannot look at them, that their hearts are "deceitful above all things" (Jer. 17:9 NIV). It does a number on your soul over time. A big piece of my work has been to help people untangle from this harmful construct and consider this truth first: *We are first and foremost made in the image of God.*

Remember the first guideline in Dignified Dialogue from the practice of listening? This applies to ourselves, too. We are first and foremost made in the image of God. In her excellent book *Original Blessing: Putting Sin in Its Rightful Place*, my friend, author and pastor Danielle Shroyer, says, "Original blessing reminds us that God calls us *good* and *beloved* before we are anything else."[5] Good and beloved. That's our starting place, our foundation, our core identity.

Part of our work in the practice of love is do what we can to call out God's beautiful image in people who don't believe it exists, who are sure that at their core they are nothing and are unworthy of love. I encounter this daily in my life at The Refuge—friends who are gender binary and nonbinary, rich and poor, evangelical and progressive, educated and uneducated and across every kind of life experience possible who do not believe they are worthy of love.

Doug, a seventy-year-old former paleontologist who went from a high paying job to driving a special needs bus making minimum wage in the last several decades, is also an orphan with no living relatives. Community is vitally important to him, and it's an honor to have journeyed with him for many years. All along, I've been trying to remind Doug that he is loved, not just with words but with presence, time, encouragement, and a long-haul relationship in community. Yet, the message that he is *unlovable* is so deeply embedded in him from a combination of childhood sexual abuse, bad theology, and painful life experiences that it is only recently that he has been able to say with a degree of confidence, "Kathy, I am actually starting to believe I am loved."

When I hear these words, I want to throw a party!

Like Doug, many of us weren't properly loved in our families of origin and suffer as adults because of it. This is why the practice of healing in chapter 1 is so crucial. We have to reckon with our own messy stories and acknowledge the truth of our brokenness and struggles in order to love more freely and fully.

When I was filled with self-loathing, self-hatred, and unforgiveness, I could still love people but it was limited and performance-based. It's what I was *supposed to do* and got praise for instead of something that flowed freely from my heart. I could offer helpful things for others, but my inability to love myself affected my ability to love my neighbor freely and fully. In the wise words of Buddhist Monk Thich Nhat Hanh, "If we do not know how to take care of ourselves and to love ourselves, we cannot take care of the people we love. Loving oneself is the foundation for loving another person."[6] For me, learning to love myself—the good, the bad, the ugly, the beautiful—has been the biggest work of my life.

Little Pockets of Love

Years ago I coined a phrase in my first solo book, *Down We Go: Living into the Wild Ways of Jesus*, that I draw back on often: *little pockets of love.*[7] Little pockets of love are some kind of space or place where people experience love in a significant way—tangibly, practically, or in deep places of their life and experience. The term first came to me after watching the movie *Precious*, the story of a young black woman healing from an abusive family trying to find her way and experiencing a safe pocket of love through a small posse of support. It's a hard and brutal movie that I highly recommend because it points to the reality that I see almost daily in the life of The Refuge—the need for people, spaces, and places to *receive* and *give* love freely.

When I first met my friend Lynette she was hardened, protective, and suspicious of me. When you are an abuse survivor and have spent your entire life being used, it's hard to receive any kind of tenderness. She said something I'll never forget when I asked who was a safe person in her life: "Kathy, I've never once had a person in my life that didn't want to take something from me. Ever. This is the first time and I still can't quite get my head around it. You mean you really don't want anything from me?" This is not unique to her; many have only been someone to use or abuse, a *project*, or someone to evangelize or help. Over a long period of time we were able to create a little pocket of love for her, but it didn't come fast or easy.

Have you ever been part of a little pocket of love personally? Created one intentionally or unintentionally? I've been part of many different expressions over the years. The Refuge is one of them, but there are so many unique forms—in houses, pubs, coffee shops, the streets, recovery meetings, homeless shelters, schools, churches, workplaces, social clubs, advocacy groups, neighborhood gatherings. The core elements of a little pocket of love are the same, regardless of the context—people can bring their real stories, hearts, struggles, pain, joy, and vulnerable lives to the table and experience love.

As we ponder the practice of love, the question for all of us is this: *How can we be cultivators of a little pocket of love in our own contexts?* What if we could be the cultivators, creators, sustainers, and nurturers of little pockets of love in all kinds of unique and creative ways? In a world filled with shame, disconnection, loneliness, and pain, love is desperately needed. Remember, love doesn't have to be complicated or big or understood by observers. Jean Vanier, who recently died at the age of 90 after a lifetime of cultivating L'Arche communities around the world where the disabled and abled live together in love and mutuality, is my favorite practictioner of love. He reminds us, "Love doesn't mean doing extraordinary or heroic things. It means knowing how to do ordinary things with tenderness."[8]

Diminishing and Growing in Love

As we close this chapter, may we remember that no matter how loving we *think* we are, there's always room to grow. Adapted from some work I've shared about safe people and communities over the years, below are ways we diminish and grow love.

Love is diminished when we:

— Think ourselves as better than others, more spiritual, more wise, more. . . .
— Focus on what we personally consider to be "right" behavior.
— Blame others instead of examining our own issues.
— Break boundaries and try to fix others.
— Pretend.
— Are inconsistent, showing up sometimes and disconnecting when it's convenient.
— Remain as the one who always "gives" and never receives.
— Place theological constructs above relationship.

Love grows when we:

— Accept others unconditionally, with no "ifs, ands, or buts."
— Help others realize their worth and value.
— Make the relationship more important than opinions.
— Give and receive in a two-way relationship.
— Are "with" each other.
— Put relationship and connection with each other above all.

— Share our own vulnerabilities and weaknesses.
— Show up consistently over the long haul
— Continually focus on the "log" (Matt. 7:3) in our own eyes.
— Offer ourselves self-compassion.

How do you connect to these? Do you have some blind spots? I sure do. Like each and every one of these practices, we will always feel like we're falling short, have work to do, that we are being challenged in ways that feel uncomfortable, messy, and even irritating.

Loving God, our neighbors, ourselves will never be a skill to be mastered or something we can measure fully. Creating pockets of love will be filled with heartbreak, annoyances, and a host of other emotional costs. But it is part of being the change we want to see in the world and embodying action that is desperately needed not only for individuals but for groups and systems as well.

The late Eugene Peterson's translation of 1 Corinthians 13 in *The Message* comes to mind, offering a twist on the apostle Paul's words on love:

> If I speak with human eloquence and angelic ecstasy but don't love, I'm nothing but the creaking of a rusty gate. If I speak God's Word with power, revealing all his mysteries and making everything plain as day, and if I have faith that says to a mountain, "Jump," and it jumps, but I don't love, I'm nothing. If I give everything I own to the poor and even go to the stake to be burned as a martyr, but I don't love, I've gotten nowhere. So, no matter what I say, what I believe, and what I do, I'm bankrupt without love.
> 1 Cor. 13:1–3 *The Message*

We're bankrupt without love.

The practice of love will challenge and transform us, and as we move into the practice of including, we will see how these practices all bleed into one another. When we're not fully included, it's hard to feel loved.

A PRAYER FOR LOVING

God, we know we're bankrupt without love.
Help us grow in love for you, our neighbors, ourselves.
If we can't love 100, we're committed to at least loving one.
Amen.

FOR PERSONAL REFLECTION

1. How can you extend love to yourself and be more gentle with your own story right now?
2. What internal message do you carry that makes it hard to love yourself? (I am . . .)
3. What story were you told about conditions that needed to be met in order for God to love you? (God loves me when I . . . if I . . .)
4. Have you heard the "love the sinner, hate the sin" phrase before? Have you personally said it? Has that drawn you toward people or away from them? How?
5. Have you ever experienced a little pocket of love? What was (or is) that like for you?

FOR GROUP REFLECTION

1. Consider the idea of a *corrective experience*, an "encounter that somehow heals, repairs, or shifts a previous trauma, assumption, or wound." Have you had a corrective experience in your own life? Share with the group what it was like for you.
2. Flesh out your feelings on *loving God first*. Is it necessary? Why or why not?
3. Why do you think it's easier to love others than yourself?
4. Who are some neighbors that are hard to love? Be honest. Do you know your actual physical neighbors? Who else do you consider neighbors?
5. What is *a little pocket of love* to which you're currently connected? If you're not, what's one you'd like to consider forming or is on your heart to cultivate?

THE PRACTICE OF LOVE

1. What do you love about yourself? This is a hard exercise but worth doing. List these things in a tangible way. Start with at least five and try to go to twenty or even higher. Own them.
2. Consider someone in your life who is difficult to love. How can you offer them love, either in relationship or in your heart to start?
3. Who around you needs love? Ask God to show you, with new eyes, areas of need. Pondering Mother Teresa's words — "If you can't feed 100 people, just feed one" — who might be the one that's tugging on your heart to feed, to honor, to love this week? Listen to the pull and make it happen. Afterward, notice: What was it like? What was hard or good?

4. Connect with a "neighbor" in some way that you're not used to. Reach out, share a meal, listen, learn, open your heart to them.
5. Attend a worship service for another religious stream you haven't experienced before. Listen for common ground and beautiful differences.

DIG DEEPER

Accidental Saints: Finding God in All the Wrong People by Nadia Bolz-Weber

Becoming Human by Jean Vanier

All about Love: New Visions by bell hooks

Creating True Peace: Ending Violence in Yourself, Your Family, Your Community, and the World by Thich Nhat Hanh

Mending the Divides: Creative Love in a Conflicted World by Jon Huckins and Jer Swigert

CHAPTER 4

THE PRACTICE OF INCLUDING

In·clude— in-klood
Verb / present participle: **including**
1. To create a space that makes room for all people
2. To intentionally embrace and value differences

There is no us and them. There's only us.
— Ken Loyd, Street Pastor

"I don't want to be identified as a lesbian; I want to be identified as a human." These words will always ring in my ears, shared by a friend who lamented how the conversations about LGBTQ+ in churches were so painful. Her eyes filled with tears and her voice rattled with a mix of anger and sadness. "Why is this so hard for people to understand?"

It shouldn't be this hard.

Full inclusion for all people across sexual and gender identities, race, socioeconomics, and abilities shouldn't be a stretch, especially at tables of the Christian faith based on the teachings of Jesus, the master includer. While the early church gathered people together around radically diverse tables, a wild mix of humans touched by Jesus' message, we can't escape that much of church history points to the practices of excluding, conquering, controlling.

Right now, many battles for inclusion are being fought in families, churches, businesses, and legislatively around the world. Denominations and churches are splitting, and tensions are extremely high around full inclusion for all, especially for LGBTQ+ folks and communities of color. A movement against immigrants and Muslims has also gained momentum, not only in the United States but throughout the West right now. On a lot of political and theological levels, Jesus' call for us to be "one" with each other (John 17:11) is not how people would describe Christians these days. It's also a reason why many have exited—or are contemplating exiting—traditional Christianity. We just can't buy into a system that keeps the exclusion wheels spinning.

On the assessment tool CliftonStrengths (formerly StrengthsFinder), my number one strength is "Includer." My including ways have gotten me into trouble over the years—especially in the ministry world where there's active resistance to inclusion across socioeconomic and life experiences. This resistance is mostly from well-resourced folks. I've noticed their responses are usually the same:

How far is too far on inclusion? What's next?
I'm not like those people.
I don't feel comfortable with . . .
But what about the Bible passages that say . . . ?
How come they get to skip all the rules? It's not fair.

I have heard these and many similar phrases for decades, and all roads usually point in the same direction: *We don't like being around people who are different from us because it makes us uncomfortable.* And let's admit it: we humans are addicted to what's comfortable and known.

Including also sometimes threatens our theological convictions, which often override the practice of love. Many just can't get around what we were taught in certain churches or our families about particular groups of people or behaviors. Most everyone I know would say we need to do something to help people who are unhoused and living outside; however, I've seen what happens when folks on the margins show up in our groups and don't change fast enough or violate our norms by speaking out of turn or arriving drunk. In the same stream, I've seen people's responses to a child with special needs, a gay couple showing public affection, or a person of color who speaks a different language. Then, inclusion is a whole different story.

Insert almost any type of person who is not like us and notice what happens internally. Even though our desire is to be people of inclusion, when the rubber meets the road we often start to feel disrupted and uncomfortable and stop short. We're used to maintaining the status quo and keeping an often unspoken but sometimes overt distance from people different from us that is always easier.

There Is No Us and Them

A few weeks ago my husband, Jose, and I crawled into bed after everyone left our house after our House of Refuge meeting. House of Refuge is an eclectic group that has met weekly since our community started in 2006. Jose said what I was thinking at exactly the same time: "Oh, how I love these people!" It's a hodgepodge group gathered not around shared beliefs but shared values and bridges a wide range of differences—rich, poor, married, single, old, young, gay, straight, evangelical, progressive, highly educated, no high school diploma, conservative, liberal, gun-lover, anti-gun advocate. Everyone in the group has a chance to facilitate, which creates an interesting mix of *you never really know what you're going to get* that probably drives some people crazy but that we greatly cherish. Across all the divides, somehow, some way, everyone's included. Our invitation to community, which we read at the beginning of our gatherings, includes this important line: "At The Refuge, everyone gives, everyone receives."

My dear friend Ken Loyd is in his mid-seventies and still journeys with people who live outside in downtown Portland. With tattoos up and down his arms, a shock of white hair, and sparkling blue eyes, Ken has the kind of deep wisdom that sinks into your heart and lodges there forever. He is also incredibly astute at the art of including. His often-said words always ring in my head and heart: "There's no us and them. There's only us."

There is no us and them, there's only us.

Imagine how different the world could be if we embodied this simple truth and began to see others not as separate from us but as our true brothers, sisters, friends?

In the previous chapter on the practice of loving, I mentioned Jean Vanier, one of my most formative teachers. Several years ago, I had the privilege of doing a training for a team of L'Arche staff in Tacoma and witnessed their work of true inclusion in real life: college-educated business people spoon-feeding folks in wheelchairs with joy and young people with extreme disabilities digging in the dirt to grow food for the hungry in their community. It is something I think everyone should experience because it epitomizes *there is no us and them, only us*. All the walls between humans broken down, our shared humanity illuminated. It's seriously beautiful.

It's important to highlight that the most core value of the L'Arche community isn't that resourced people *include* disabled people. It's that the *entire community* is centered around the margins. This is key in the conversation about inclusion. If we're still working from a template based on how those in power "need to be more inclusive," the power will still remain the same and those on the margins will remain on the margins. Instead, real transformation will happen when we center ourselves around folks who are typically on the margins—depending on the group—from people of color to LGBTQ+ to women to the under-resourced financially to those living with disabilities. Centering means completely upending power structures that have been in place for generations. We can't get to centering in a flash, but we can begin to reexamine deeply entrenched positions and notice our resistance to change.

My friend Brandan Robertson is in his mid-twenties and is one of the most intelligent and challenging voices for inclusion in the church today. He identifies as queer and is a pastor, writer, and pot-stirrer. His voice always reminds me that moving the needle on true inclusion will require a level of agitation and discomfort that will some-times feel harshly tilted against those who have benefitted from excluding. In his book *True Inclusion: Creating Communities of Radical Embrace*, Brandan says,

> True inclusion demands that we recognize that only in our diversity do we more perfectly reflect the divinity of our expansive Creator. Whenever we are compelled to declare that someone doesn't belong, whether it's because of their sexuality, ethnicity, back-ground, beliefs, political affiliations, disruptiveness, neediness, inconvenience, struggles, immaturity, etc., we are dehumanizing ourselves and the one(s) we are excluding. That is an assault on the very image and likeness of God in the world.[1]

Exclusion is always about us and them, who's out, who's in, who's with us, who's against us, who's like us, who's not like us. Inclusion is about the beautiful reality of God that we're all in—we're all *us*—together.

We Love Our Walls

There's a meme that floats around Facebook in waves. It says: "When you have more than you need, build a bigger table, not a higher fence." I have trekked to the Middle East several times in the past few years, heard stories from Palestinian refugees and Israelis and saw some of the painful and overwhelming realities of the ongoing conflict between them. What's happening in the Middle East is central to conversations about equality, inclusion, and advocacy because it is a microcosm of our human tendency to scapegoat, hoard power, and exclude. Constructed by Israel, walls separate Palestinians into specific areas throughout the region. Many aren't aware that people can go into walled sections, but Palestinians can't travel freely out of their confined areas, use Israel's airport, or work without a special permit. Many of their human rights have been stripped. In a nutshell, those with power can move freely and those on the margins cannot. Yet, it gets extra tangled up because Israel has also been an oppressed people, displaced for centuries, and the victims of a horrific genocide. In the United States, the battles over a wall on the southern border with Mexico has been fanned into a raging flame, stirring up hot emotions on both sides of the issue. On a recent visit to Ireland I learned all about the "peace walls" that were constructed between Protestants and Catholics in response to violence decades ago. These walls still exist because people are used to their function. I know people who live in all three of these places committed to finding ways through these physical walls to get to the heart of who is behind them—people. God's creation, our brothers, our sisters.

Regardless of a wide range of complicated histories related to walls, for the practice of including we must consider this: *Walls are usually never built by the under-resourced.* Walls are always built by those with the most power and are about a physical separation that represents an emotional and relational segregation.

This particular book isn't about domestic or foreign policies, but it is about how these examples are showing up in our own personal lives and experiences and how we can embody something different in the world. It always starts with our own self-examination: *What walls have we constructed?* Who are we trying to keep out? Who is hard for us to include? Is this because of our own experiences or because of what we've been told by leaders or the media?

And the biggest one—*what are we afraid of?* Walls are always about exclusion built from fear.

The bottom line is that we human beings have an innate tendency to be judgers, separators, and excluders. We feel threatened by change or any disruption that may cause us to lose power. We may try to fool ourselves into thinking it's not about power, but it always is. Across all levels of humanity, the desire to get power and retain power— whether it is conscious or not—is always real and is always threaded into exclusion.

It's why we build walls.

Using God to Exclude

God's supposed to help us break down walls, but unfortunately, we often use God to help cement our case for exclusion. My friend and popular author, pastor, and social activist, John Pavlovitz, writes in his book *A Bigger Table*,

> One of the biggest, most damaging mistakes too many Christians so willingly make is assuming that God is as much of a judgmental jerk as we are. But what if we could make room for difference and space for disagreement in our spiritual communities? What if we could give permission for moral failure and freedom to not be certain, and the chance

to gloriously fail without needing those things to become black marks against people or death-penalty offenses? What if we made space for people who are as screwed up as we are?[2]

I'd add: What if we made space for people who look different, think different, believe different, act different, pray different, and vote different?

Our tables would look a lot different!

"But God says . . . " or "The Bible says . . ." are two of the most powerful weapons to keep our friends and family excluded, separated by walls, or uninvited to certain tables. In her book *Inspired: Slaying Giants, Walking on Water, and Loving the Bible Again,* my friend and beloved best-selling author, Rachel Held Evans, who tragically died while I was writing this book, reminds us: "The apostles remembered what many modern Christians tend to forget — that what makes the gospel offensive isn't who it keeps out but who it lets in."[3]

What makes the gospel offensive isn't who it keeps out but who it lets in.

Who were you taught wasn't worthy to sit at certain tables? Who do you subtly or directly think should be excluded because of what they believe or don't believe? What groups were you taught to be afraid of or that you needed to *pray for?*

Rachel was a prophet for inclusion, a wall-breaker, table-maker, and a champion for those who were usually kept out, left out. Sometimes the keeping out is overt, and at other times it's sneakier.

Have you ever had the experience of having to sit at the rickety card table set up in the overflow space for a special holiday meal at your grandparents' house? It's for the people who can't fit at the nice table, like the kids or latecomers to the party. To me, the rickety card table set up during a special holiday dinner represents getting the scraps, a sometimes subtle, sometimes direct message that says, *We're glad you came, but there's really no room for you to sit with us at the real table. You are part of the B team.* Many people I intersect with are used to sitting at the card table. They've always lived on the margins socioeconomically, practically, spiritually, and in other ways. They've never been invited to the big table — ever.

As people of faith and practice, we should be the biggest table-makers in town! Our tables should have room for everyone — the fringe, the lonely, doubters, pious believers, poor, rich, educated, uneducated, men, women, nonbinary, gay, straight, black, white, brown, young, old, liberal, conservative, and everything in between. We can always add more leaves to make the table bigger and pull up more chairs. Around tables is where our shared humanity emerges, where we can listen, learn, and find that although we seem so different, we're all really longing for the same things — to love and be loved, to give and receive.

It makes me circle back to my dear friend's comment at the beginning: "I don't want to be identified as a lesbian; I want to be identified as a human."

Exclusion is dehumanizing. The core practice of including is respecting the human dignity of all people, God's image embedded in each and every person.

For a lot of us, we don't actively try to exclude. However, we remain comfortable and safe in our protected lives and faith communities and don't even recognize how homogeneous our experiences are — surrounded by people who look, think, and believe like us. My long-time friend Ann is a white, middle-class, former physical therapist who raised three kids in the suburbs and has an infectious smile and gentle spirit. She often shares how her world has been expanded through The Refuge as an inclusive community but how hard it can be here, too, after spending many years in traditional churches:

> Sometimes I miss what my life was like before, where I knew what to expect. But I also felt like I had

stopped growing. Now, every time I'm sitting beside people completely different from me, listening and learning and sharing life together, I am amazed at how much I was missing. Sometimes I love it, other times I hate it, but one thing is always true—I am continually transformed.

The questions we all need to keep wrestling with in our own unique circumstances are: What is God stirring up in us about inclusion and how can we bravely move toward something that is a better reflection of God's heart for all people? We won't get to a new place without some radical shifts in our practices. I think if Jesus was here teaching in the flesh again, he'd be turning over tables, clearing out churches, and raising some serious ruckus over how we are not only missing the point but are continuing to damage far too many people in the name of God.

Welcome Is Not Inclusion

"All are welcome here" is a sign that most every church waves or what most people like to think about themselves in relationship. We want to be people of welcome.

However, welcome is not the same as inclusion. Welcome says, "Come on in, come eat with us, be with us, converse with us, hang out with us . . . but (and there's always a *but*) in order to be fully included you have to believe, act, and be a certain way."

The practice of including moves beyond a false welcome into being people who foster equal, meaningful, interconnected relationships across all our differences.

Those who struggle with mental illness and physical disabilities are often the most excluded and ostracized and easily ignored in conversations about inclusion. I have a friend who has been asked to leave multiple communities because he didn't properly follow the norms in ways that made some people uncomfortable. Other friends had children with disabilities and were asked to keep them quiet or make impossible adjustments so others wouldn't be bothered. When I hear these stories, I want to scream! Being people of inclusion means that we honor the disruptions, real, messy, and loud as the beauty of our humanity together—not something to be squeezed out so that the more resourced feel comfortable.

I love the Mama Bears, a group of passionate moms who have LGBTQ+ kids and actively work to advocate on their behalf. Many come from rigid or conservative faith systems that actively exclude their children and were forced to make a choice—our kid or the church? Thankfully, they chose their kids.

My friend Liz Dyer was part of a conservative evangelical church in the heart of Texas for years. When her son came out as gay years ago, she ended up losing her church, community, and faith as she once knew it. Now a passionate advocate for equality, Liz leads an online Facebook group of over 7,500 moms of LGBTQ+ kids and is a wonderfully fierce voice in my life and many others around the globe. Years ago, I was in painful conversations with my ministry partner over our differing views on same-sex marriage at The Refuge. I kept my eyes squarely on all my kids, who will not tolerate exclusion of any kind, but especially my son Jared, who was passionate about inclusion not only for himself but for all people. During this season, Liz shared lasting words on the difference between welcome and inclusion, and how important it is for groups and individuals to be clear on the difference. Churches can say, "We welcome everyone," but if certain people can't lead freely, marry freely, participate freely, it's not somewhere that a person on the underside of power will ever flourish. A good question to ask is, "Who is allowed to lead in your church?" Church Clarity is a helpful website that rates Christian congregations on policies of inclusion — not vague statements of welcome. It formed to force churches to be more clear about inclusion in their communities and is worth checking out.

Welcome is about open doors. It says, "Sure you can be you as part of *us*, but with certain conditions that limit." Inclusion is about fully open tables and hearts where there is only *us, unconditionally, period.*

Part of the practice of inclusion is recognizing this difference.

Some Denver friends at a local mega-church tackled the practice of LGBTQ+ inclusion with grace and perseverance several years ago. Moving from a traditional evangelical framework that used the words "welcome" to a more progressive one that allowed for full inclusion for all was no small task but is part of the wave of greater societal inclusion that's happening today. I watched them labor, learn, and lament together as part of their process over several years, giving everyone a chance to use their voice and wrestle toward a better way together. In the end, they lost some people who couldn't reconcile their theological convictions with full inclusion and took a hit with some of their donor base. However, they transformed themselves into a more free and integrated community and have earned the respect of many in our city. They took a stand on the side of love and inclusion. And it mattered.

On a larger scale, the United Methodists are in the middle of a painful process right now with the realities of the deep theological divides in their denomination. It's causing extreme damage to many pastors and members who had hoped for a way to live together as *us* despite the differences. Their story is being played out, and we don't know the next trajectory it will all take, but we do know this: it's causing incredible pain to many.

However, some of our biggest work in the practice of including can be shifting our energy from pointing the finger at which groups or people are *not* including to being the ones who are. Any conversation and challenge related to inclusion is incomplete without talking about scapegoating and how finger pointing is extremely natural to us.

How We Love to Scapegoat

The 2016 presidential election in the United States and Donald Trump's rise to political power revealed divisions in our culture that a lot of people knew existed but that had previously remained unexposed. Social media and the rise of interconnectedness and nonstop news flooding into our phones and houses has helped each of us engage in ways that are different from previous seasons of civil unrest in our history. As painful as it is, it's a good thing. I have never seen more people involved and active in civic engagement. People realized, some for the first time, that there's a high price to pay for apathy. It's no surprise that while I am friends and in community with people across the spectrum of theological beliefs and political persuasions, surviving this kind of presidency has been brutally difficult for me personally, with a relentless assault on people and issues I deeply value.

What's happened in the United States is not unique; it has revealed a classic pattern evident in most every culture and group that is extremely important in conversations about the practice of including—scapegoating.

Scapegoating is the inappropriate placing of blame on another person or group in an effort to gain power or relief from our own pain. Scapegoating individuals and groups is one of the greatest detriments to including, and most all humans are guilty of it. Scapegoating helps us appear better than another; it helps us cope with the tension we don't know how to resolve except through the violent act of making *the other* the enemy. All of scapegoating is about avoiding our own pain. It reminds me of author, playwright, and civil rights activist James Baldwin's telling words, "I imagine one of the reasons people cling to their hates so stubbornly is because they sense, once hate is gone, they will be forced to deal with pain."[4]

Once hate is gone, we will be forced to deal with pain.

We humans are masters at separating, turning against, withdrawing, blaming, pointing the finger, circling our wagons, and placing ourselves as superior to others—all in an effort to protect ourselves from pain and save our own skin. Scapegoating protects individuals and groups from looking at our own dysfunction.

French anthropologist René Girard has done extensive work around scapegoating that is worth examining more intentionally. In its simplest form it centers on individuals and groups who find a way to gather around "who's out" and use whatever measures necessary to scapegoat them. Shame, blame, forcing out, and ostracizing are usually key ingredients.

In Girard's well-researched Mimetic Theory,[5] he nailed a critical point about human nature—our innate tendency toward violence and separation from others. Violence doesn't always look like guns, bombs, and physical assault. Violence often looks like turning against our brothers, sisters, ourselves, and God to protect ourselves. This can come out in all kinds of different ways that are far subtler than war. Emotional violence is one of the most prevalent and causes deep damage to not only its victims but ultimately to its perpetrators too.

Most of us have both scapegoated others and been the scapegoat, often in the same system. Years ago when I worked on an extremely unhealthy mega-church staff, I was part of a form of emotional violence toward a fellow teammate. When I look back on it, I got sucked into the things people said about her, how she wasn't a good fit, and it would be best for everyone if she left. I remember coming to work one morning to her emptied office and the staff team carrying forward without skipping a beat. In the short term, I felt better. Our leadership team did feel easier, and I could justify in my mind why it was a good decision—for a little while. Then, a chunk of months later, I got to walk in her shoes. I was next to become the topic of closed-door conversations, the one queued up to be excluded. The same pattern lasted a few months, and I found myself on the outs also. After being asked to resign and pulling myself up off the floor, one of the first things I did was invite her to lunch and apologize for my blindness and contribution to the violence against her. It was a lovely and healing conversation, and we remain connected all these years later. Still, I am sad at how easily I embraced a subtle and duplicitous scapegoating that harmed, divided, and perpetuated violence.

In the conversation on including, we must consider the groups we are part of and who we might like to collectively scapegoat. Who do we judge and separate from? Who are we most afraid of? Who do we think we are better than? On a more personal level, what is a group or type of person you feel emotional violence against? Is it religious conservatives? Family members? A particular kind of protestor or activist? Those who believe particular things contrary to you?

In The Refuge community, the spirit of inclusion is high and something the community has celebrated—with one big exception. If someone is religiously conservative, they can feel very excluded. I am not proud of this. I confess that part of my healing has been to notice my reflex tendency to scapegoat conservative Christians. If you identify as a conservative evangelical and are reading this, I am sorry for the ways I have lumped you into a group I made my common enemy. With a long history of real and valid pain from the evangelical stream related to inclusion for many years, I recognize I have often become the excluder, scapegoating and replicating violence in a different form. I've tried to make my amends and model something different in these past few years, but I know there's still ongoing work to do to embody a healthier way.

Taking the easy road of scapegoating will always deflect us from the deeper work we need to do. It is the antithesis of inclusion. Our best hope in the practice of including is to identify this violent and powerful human tendency and do the hard and humble work of repenting from it, refusing to rely on it to ease our own anxiety and pain. In our current political and theological climates around the world built with hostility and division, refusing to participate in scapegoating others is even more critical. Jesus, the one who refused to return violence for violence, models the way for us. It's a high bar, but if we just start with that one place—refusing to return violence for violence—we'll make some headway.

Ways We Exclude, Ways We Include

While the practice of including is played out in groups and systems, it's also very personal and can happen in ordinary ways in our everyday lives. Individually, we can practice including by being people who reach out to others and find our common humanity in different ways in the small circles we live and move in. We can invite others to sit at our tables and share stories. We can raise our head up from our workstation and pause to draw in a coworker on a human level. We can be the ones who sit next to others who are by themselves in the cafeteria, at church, or in a social situation. We can share what we're talking about when a new person joins the conversation so they're not left out to dry. We can use people's preferred pronouns. We can make horseshoes instead of closed circles.

We can develop ears and eyes to notice: Who's alone? Who's excluded? Who's quiet? Who's extra annoying? Who do we disagree with the most? Who's the one at first glance that you probably want to connect with least? Who am I tempted to scapegoat or avoid? Who am I somehow afraid of?

Then, in whatever ways we can, we move toward them. Whether we're introverts, extroverts, young, old, well-resourced, under-resourced, attend church, or are allergic to religion, if we want the world to be a better place, we've all got to play our part in including.

I want to end this chapter with some differences between excluders and includers so we can see ourselves in each of these broad movements and identify specific areas to keep practicing. It's easy to keep the conversation up high and lose sight of the changes we need to make personally and in our groups. Even for the most passionate, progressive, inclusionary folks, we likely exclude and scapegoat and can be blinded by our call. The lists I created below are for all of us in our own distinctive ways. No one is exempt. Our work in being healthier humans and changing the world for good requires contemplation and introspection.

Think through who is hard for you, who you naturally want to exclude, who's been rattling around in your head and heart as you've been reading this chapter. Read some attributes of exclusion below. When you're honest, which do you know you tend to do?

We exclude by:
- ❏ Defining others by what they believe or do.
- ❏ Staying comfortable and not wanting to get our hands dirty.
- ❏ Following what leaders say about particular people or groups.
- ❏ Building walls in our hearts against certain types of people.
- ❏ Assuming our interpretation of faith texts is the only right way.
- ❏ Fostering fear of the other in various ways.
- ❏ Remaining in homogeneous circles where we don't have a chance to listen and learn from people different from us.
- ❏ Refusing to be open to feedback or constructive criticism or a change in our position.

❏ Believing we are somehow superior in our knowledge, belief, passion, or actions.
❏ People-pleasing, toeing the line, and remaining in exclusionary systems even when inside we know that it's violating our integrity.
❏ Scapegoating people and groups to separate ourselves from pain and difference.
❏ Protecting our power.

Now consider what the Spirit has been stirring up in you and read some characteristics of inclusion below. What resonates as an area you know you'd love to work on practicing in the months ahead? Which of these are hardest for you? Easiest?

We include by:
❏ Seeing beyond beliefs and affiliations.
❏ Living with discomfort and a willingness to engage in messy relationships.
❏ Thinking for ourselves and refusing to blindly follow what others tell us about people or groups.
❏ Doing the hard work of brutally honest self-reflection related to our fears and biases.
❏ Sitting at tables across differences and listening, and listening some more.
❏ Keeping the wild ways of Jesus at the forefront.
❏ Practicing courage to expand our hearts and minds.
❏ Joining in on conversations, learning and serving opportunities that expand our limited vision.
❏ Remaining humble, open to feedback, constructive criticism, and shifting our positions.
❏ Integrating *there is no us and them, only us* into our deepest experiences.
❏ Telling the truth about our convictions and risking the disapproval of others.

❏ Building bridges across vast divides while remaining authentic about our positions and passions.
❏ Releasing our power to make room for under-represented power to emerge.

The practice of including will always be met with resistance and will always cost us something. I love knowing so many of you are willing to pay the price with your time, jobs, ego, position. You know what's at stake. You know there's no going back to the status quo. You're clear you can no longer be part of systems that exclude. You've had enough talking about including and just want to play your part in actually living it out.

That's what a life of practice is all about.

As we move on to the practice of equalizing, remember all of these practices are tangled up together. They each will require much of us. We won't be able to master any of them, but our work isn't about mastery. It's about being a participant in change as best we can. Including and equalizing are different but they are also intimately connected.

A PRAYER FOR INCLUDING

God, help us become people and practitioners of inclusion.
Heal our insecurities, fears, and self-protections.
Give us courage to widen tables, break down walls, open doors, and
*   expand hearts.*
Strengthen and free us from our reflex to scapegoat others as an
*   easy way out.*
Amen.

FOR PERSONAL REFLECTION

1. What group(s) or types of people are hardest to include? Who are the *thems* in your life?
2. Consider what walls you might have constructed toward other people or particular groups. What do these walls look or feel like? Are some of them breaking down in this season? How?
3. How would you describe the difference between welcome and inclusion? Have you felt the difference in your own experience?
4. Consider the idea of scapegoating. How have you scapegoated others? Been scapegoated? How did those experiences feel?
5. What feels hard about the practice of inclusion?

FOR GROUP REFLECTION

1. Reflect on the major movements in this chapter— there is no us and them, using God to exclude, we love our walls, scapegoating, and how we exclude and include. What especially resonated? In what areas were you challenged?
2. How have you been part of groups that have excluded others? Who were those groups? What do you regret about that? What are you trying to do differently?
3. Every group is a microcosm of the bigger story; remember it's not always about who *isn't* at the table but how those who are really feel. With a desire to keep strengthening the health of this group, how can you practice inclusion in new ways? What's

missing? How do you sometimes feel? Try to be as honest and specific as you can.

4. As you reflect on the idea of scapegoating, think of a concrete example where you have either scapegoated others or been scapegoated or both. What feelings does it stir up in you? Knowing what you know now, what could you do differently?

5. Consider the list of ways we exclude and include and note which you most identify with, either as something you tend to do or hope to cultivate more of in your practice. Share any reflections with the group.

FOR PRACTICE

1. Think of the tables you are currently sitting at in your work, family, church, community. How can you put in some leaves and pull up more chairs to better include others? Do it.

2. Challenge the system you are in by having conversations about inclusion with leadership or others in the group. Rock the boat and notice the resistance and your fear.

3. Listen to a story from someone who has been excluded. Sit with the reality of their experience and consider what is stirred in your heart through it.

4. As you review some of the ways we can include, choose one you want to work on and find a tangible way to practice it in your real life.

5. If it doesn't harm yourself or others, make amends to someone you scapegoated, either in a real-life conversation or through some kind of written communication. Share your heart and what you were afraid of and how you would do it differently if you could.

6. Volunteer at an organization dedicated to people who are often excluded for different reasons and integrate what you learn into your vocabulary and experience.

DIG DEEPER

A Bigger Table: Building Messy, Authentic, and Hopeful Spiritual Community by John Pavlovitz

True Inclusion: Creating Communities of Radical Embrace by Brandan Robertson

Unashamed: A Coming-Out Guide for LGBTQ Christians by Amber Cantorna

Wild Mercy: Living the Fierce and Tender Wisdom of the Women Mystics by Mirabai Starr

CHAPTER 5

———————

THE PRACTICE OF
EQUALIZING

E·qua·lize—ee-kwuh-lahyz
Verb / present participle: **equalizing**
1. To level imbalances between people or things
2. To create consistency across differences
3. To intentionally dismantle inequalities

*Reconciliation requires imagination. It requires looking
beyond what is to what could be. It looks beyond intentions
to real outcomes, real hurts, real histories.*[1]
　　　　　　　　　　　—Austin Channing Brown

I want you to start this chapter by pausing for a moment.
Close your eyes and reflect on this simple question: Are all
people equal?

Are all people equal?

What came to mind? What's your first response to this
question? It probably depends on who you are and how
much power you hold in the world. Sure, most of us want
to be able to say yes. We want to believe we are equal.

We want to hope we are. We might even default to what a lot of people of faith say: "We're all equal in the sight of God." If your life is lived on the underside of power because of race, gender, sexual orientation, socioeconomics, or abilities, you probably are the first to say, "Are you freaking kidding me? Of course we're not equal. Everyone knows that."

Yes, unfortunately, God's heart and real life are often two different things.

That's what this chapter is about.

To me, equalizing is one of the most core practices in a transformational life. The practice of equalizing and including have a lot of overlap, but I like to distinguish them this way: Including is about actively integrating all of us together—individuals and groups—as a life practice. The practice of equalizing is about recognizing and working to shift disparate power for under-empowered groups. At the core of equalizing is the belief that every human has equal, full, unequivocal dignity and worth alongside every other human.

Equal, full, unequivocal dignity and worth alongside every other human.

Equalizing isn't about cookie-cutter humanity, where we are all the exactly the same. We know we're not, and that's part of the beauty of the human family. Rather, equalizing is about honoring our unique distinctions—across all of the power divides created by humans—and creating a way of seeing, moving, and being in the world that reflects the core truth that every human has equal, full, unequivocal dignity and worth alongside every other human. We'll keep coming back to this.

This, my friends, is rough work that continues to be met with great resistance, not only from outside forces but also from the dark crevices in our heart and experience. No matter how processed or enlightened we think we are, we are actually participants in inequality, racism, sexism, able-ism, and a host of other sneaky ways we act as if some people are worth less than others. The practice of equalizing requires that we look at the forces at work in the world, our own personal experiences, and our shared history that have caused severe damage to generations of people and that we will probably spend our lifetimes untangling from.

As we work through this chapter together, please know we can only cover so much ground in 6,000 words. We're going to go for a deep dive, and we'll also only barely scratch the surface. You will feel both. Remember, this book is about a mix of tangible practices that change us to change the world. For equalizing, the Dig Deeper list is longer for a reason. We've got a lot of catching up to do on equalizing, and these harmful power divides are not going to heal easily. Despite the many limitations, my hope is that we engage in this chapter together as humbly and openly as we can, gleaning what we each need to be challenged by in our own unique ways for our own particular groups.

On Earth as It Is in Heaven

The evidence throughout history and culture suggests that full equality among people will not happen naturally. Due to our most basic survival instincts embedded inside us, human beings have a propensity toward an imbalance of power. It's just what humans do. Almost every story— from our ancient biblical texts to the teachings of Jesus to mythology to movies being made today—reflect this part of our humanity. It's not that it never occurs on its own, but without serious work and intention, our natural human defaults are toward inequality, separation, one-up and one-down-ness.

Take a look at the first image below. In this position, one group or person is *greater than* and the other *less*. These hands represent not only individual relationships but also groups and systems that operate in the over or under duality. They embody inequality.

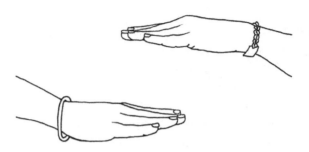

Now think about the kingdom of God that Jesus spoke of in what most call the Lord's Prayer in Matthew 6. "Your kingdom come. Your will be done, on earth as it is in heaven" (v. 10). Jesus was reminding us that this reality of God here, now, is possible. Is this disparity really what heaven looks like? Over and under, some more, some less? One group more valuable than another?

I'm not certain of much, but I'll stake my claim that heaven looks like this:

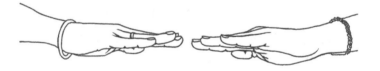

Every wall broken down, all the divides bridged, all equal.

On earth as it is in heaven.

But let's be honest. Some people's faith is what drives them to perpetuate inequality. Their view of heaven is that a whole bunch of people are truly *less than* and are unworthy to be there. Christian superiority runs rampant, and deeply entrenched in so many of our systems is the thought that white cisgender Western males are somehow better than everyone else. Please know that I completely denounce this as sin. Its insidious nature has and will continue to ruin unless we embody and cultivate something different in our hearts, practices, and systems. The kind of heaven on earth I'm talking about is where every human being has equal, full, unequivocal dignity and worth alongside every other human.

Much will be required of us as people committed to equalizing.

Years ago, I was at a conference hosted by Father Richard Rohr's organization—Center for Action and Contemplation—in New Mexico centered on possibilities for a more imaginative and inclusive church. One of the speakers was Alexia Torres-Fleming, an amazingly gifted Latinx community organizer from the Bronx in New York who spoke about shifts they were working toward in their neighborhood, riffing off Ezekiel 37 and the passages centered on dry bones coming to life. Her impassioned speech still rings in my ears, and her words have lingered for years: "The kingdom of God isn't going to just drop out of the sky."

The kingdom isn't going to just drop out of the sky.

Equality won't, either.

New life, hope, and change aren't going to magically drop on our doorstep because we wish for it, long for it, pray for it, share memes on Facebook about it. As much as we all want it to come quickly, we are not going to wake up anytime soon with equal tables, equal voices, equal leadership, equal dignity, equal rights.

We—in all our flawed, beautiful, failing, and flailing ways—are tasked with being the ones who work to create it. We'll also be working on it our entire lifetimes (and our children will be working on it after us). We need courage to act not once, not twice, but over the long story. Margaret Wheatley, organizational sociologist, author, and powerful voice for individual and systems change, says, "The greatest source of courage is to realize that if we don't act, nothing will change for the better. Reality doesn't change itself. It needs us to act."[2]

Equality Requires Creativity

My dad was a true-blue hippy during the 1960s and early '70s. My parents were divorced when I was five years old, and I have treasured memories of selling spoon rings on the streets of Berkeley and meeting peace-lovers who put daisies in my hair at the park. Part of that culture was a desire for social change. As I grew up, I was the kid who would join causes—save the whales, equal rights for women, and the American Civil Liberties Union (ACLU). After graduating high school, I ended up in a conservative Christian college on a scholarship and became immersed in a radically different culture where being a Democrat and advocating for certain causes was often considered akin to sin.

As time went on and I started attending church more regularly, I switched my political affiliation to Republican, tore up my ACLU membership card, and began to see the world as something I should escape from as a Christian. For years, my advocacy work was not on behalf of the poor, marginalized, and discriminated, but rather to rally against Harry Potter books and the lack of prayer in school. Now, it's embarrassing, but I have to own it as part of my story. Plus, I'm guessing I might be in good company with some of you who have also radically changed with time, experience, and a shifting faith.

For the past fifteen years I have become a more vocal activist for equality. My shift looked a lot like Paul's conversion story in Acts 9 with the scales falling off Saul's eyes and seeing things completely differently and becoming forever changed. For years, I didn't recognize the blaring inequality in the church cultures I served in until some people questioned why I was so undervalued and underutilized. I had been taught to be *under* leadership and suppressed the hunger for equality because it represented self-centeredness that as a "good Christian woman" I was supposed to guard against. I had become conditioned to toe the line, submit to authority, and not rock the boat.

As I began to see patriarchy, hierarchy, and sexism more clearly, I ended up losing my job as an adult ministry pastor at a local mega-church. My separation was over two primary issues—first, advocating for full equality and value for people on the margins who struggled with addictions, mental illness, poverty, abuse, and other human struggles; and then the church being challenged to state their theological position on women having teaching authority after I preached at a weekend service. Some of you who are in mainline denominations might be laughing since you have had female pastors in the upper levels of leadership for many years. If you consider yourself a *None* related to spiritual affiliation or *Done* with church, you are probably rolling your eyes at yet another example of why you left. There's no question that churches are some of the most unequal places on the planet, with much of our infrastructure and culture built on hierarchical, exclusive systems that thrive on an *over/under* dynamic, and covert control.

Over the years there has been change, albeit not nearly enough. There are indeed more women in church and business leadership than ever before. Same-sex marriage is now legal, and 2018 brought the most racially diverse U.S. Congress in history. These are all things to celebrate but let us never forget—we have a long way to go to get to full equality for all.

As I grew in a more practical faith and intersected intimately not only with my own story but with more people living in poverty and pain, my eyes and heart were awakened in new ways. I began to notice the inequality of systems, how people with privilege and power could easily open doors but those without it would never be able to catch a break. I witnessed how biased people were against the poor and would make false assumptions about their character. I saw how women were subjugated underneath men in countless contexts and how racism was rampant.

Mostly, I noticed how most systems are unjust against those on the margins and how Jesus was all about turning that upside down. Our faith isn't just for us. It's fuel for creating a new reality for people who are hungry, hurting, and marginalized, for restoring dignity and hope where it's been lost, for bringing the good news into hard places, for righting the tilted systems that are unfairly biased. It's not about only advocating for equality, but active participation in prophetically creating it.

Equalizing will require creative justice. Years ago, I stumbled on a helpful image that considers the difference between superficial equality and healing justice. My talented artist friend Amy Jo Nova drew it this way:

Do you see the difference? What does it stir up in you?

I have read various critiques of the image, particularly pointing out that the second image misses the ultimate goal of liberation—where the walls are completely broken down and the three would have seats inside the stadium. But the takeaway worth considering is how unique, creative, and imaginative we must be in our practices of equalizing. One size doesn't fit all. Policies alone won't cut it. Quick Band-Aid fixes and asking a few women, people of color, or LGBTQ+ folks to be on our teams won't do it. Opening doors on systemic cages and expecting people to simply fly out of them isn't remotely a possibility without meaningful relational work that paves the way.

A good forward step in the practice of equalizing includes a painful self-awareness and historical awareness so we can be honest about what we're up against. When we begin to look at the deep grooves of inequality it can become overwhelming and sometimes even feel hopeless. Still, we must push through our discomfort and insecurities and have our souls and practices rocked so we can become agents of change. In the words of black author and activist James Baldwin, "Any real change implies the breakup of the world as one has always known it, the loss of all that gave one an identity, the end of safety."[3]

Part of the practice of equalizing is giving up safety and the world as we knew it.

Privilege Is a Good Place to Start

Any conversation on equalizing also needs to include some honest processing of *privilege*. Peggy McIntosh, anti-racism author and speaker, defines privilege this way: "Privilege exists when one group has something of value that is denied to others simply because of the groups they belong to, rather than because of anything they've done or failed to do."[4] My friend Michelle Warren, who is an author, public policy advocate, and a white woman living in a low-income Latinx community in central Denver, recently said it this way at a workshop gathering at The Refuge: "Privilege is the ability to opt out." *Privilege* doesn't have to be a dirty word and can't be if we're going to become practitioners of equality. Let me say it louder for the people in the back—we don't have to be ashamed to admit that we benefit from privilege. The more we acknowledge, wrestle, engage, process, and get it out on the table honestly, the more transformation is possible.

Privilege comes in many forms — male, white, straight, educational, economic, religious, ability, and more — and always centers on certain people having access that other people do not have. Talking about privilege often feels like a violation of the white, Protestant work-ethic value that our country is founded on. We want to believe everyone has the same shot and that everyone starts at the same place.

It's just not true.

As a white, married, straight woman with a master's degree, I am extremely privileged. Yet, a lot of people don't know that my dad was an alcoholic who only made it through ninth grade, and my mom was a single mom struggling daily to pay the bills. I was on loads of financial aid and scholarships and worked every day to pay my way through college. Regardless of how hard my education was to get and how much we struggled financially growing up, I must still own and never minimize: *I am extremely privileged and carry inherent power because of it.*

Our bristling, defensiveness, and protectiveness around privilege creates harmful denial. It's painful to talk honestly about our jacked-up systems and the ways many of us have benefitted while others have suffered. It's painful to talk about the ways we have huddled in our churches and homogeneous groups and protected ourselves from the realities that are now making their way into our living room TVs and Facebook feeds at a rapid rate. It's painful to acknowledge how little we actually know about peacemaking and participating in systemic transformation after years and decades of "going to church." It's painful to begin to bear the burden of our brothers and sisters without privilege and embrace their stories as part of ours and honor how our freedom is all tied up together, and that there are huge knots to untangle.

But we must.

My friend Ramón, who is black and Puerto Rican, lives in a predominantly white neighborhood in North Denver.

Now a multicultural therapist for people on the margins socioeconomically, for many years he learned how to play by the rules in white Christian culture, which mandated that he not bring up issues of inequality or talk about tough topics like privilege, white supremacy, and institutional oppression. In many Christian circles, "privilege" and "white supremacy" are usually some of the most provoking.

He says it's because of the reality that whiteness is normative in American Christianity (think of how we toss around the labels "Black Church" or "Chinese Church" as a start). Those who are white resist acknowledging this. This resistance makes sense. He adds,

> In short, who wants to be Pharaoh? Who wants to believe their country is Babylon? Every narrative in the scriptures is opposed to Empire, yet white Christians have largely used the scriptures to support white supremacy—missionary colonists, Manifest Destiny, slavery, segregation, Indian boarding schools, anti-Semitism. I think white Christians are resistant to acknowledging "privilege" and "white supremacy" because those concepts make it clear that white Christian history is clearly at odds with the prophetic tradition that proclaims God stands on the side of the oppressed.

Ramón hits this nail on the head.

To repent from our resistance to these important conversations, we are going to have to put down our swords, defenses, pride, protections, fears, and justifications and ask God to move in our lives. To turn our hearts of stone into hearts of flesh. To help the scales fall off our eyes. To repent from the false theologies we have followed. To allow our souls to be stirred and live in the discomfort because transformation never happens in the comfortable.

These are some of the reasons you probably picked up this book on practice and are traveling this road with me.

We know as people of privilege we've got a lot to learn. The way forward starts with tender humility and brutal honesty about the history Ramón just challenged us to consider.

Owning the Lie of White Supremacy

For you who are white like me, I have a special message when it comes to issues of equality that's centered on race: In addition to acknowledging our embedded privilege, we have a responsibility to own our inherent place in the lie of white supremacy and the damage it has done and continues to do in our culture.

We can't wiggle our way out of it — we are stewed in the lie of white supremacy from our earliest childhood. Part of the practice of equalizing is owning it. I told you from the beginning this book would make us uncomfortable. If we want to be the change we want to see in the world, we must be disrupted, rattled, shaken, moved, and transformed. It starts with us and — in the words of the fourth step in recovery — "a fearless moral inventory of ourselves." My friend Sage, who has been part of The Refuge since we first started, is currently working on a Twelve-step path for white people to directly face the ravages of colonialism. He modified the fourth step to read: "Made a searching and fearless moral inventory of ourselves and of our history."

Owning our place in the lie of white supremacy isn't about dramatically beating ourselves up for our racial sins and the sins of our ancestors; it's about acknowledging, out loud and in the buried places of our hearts, how we have benefitted from the powerful systems of whiteness that have not only colonized and infiltrated the United States of America but every pocket, nook, and cranny around the globe. If you are a person of color reading this, everything I say will be limited because of my perspective as a white person living in America, and I acutely know it. My role in this section is to speak to my white brothers and sisters. Hopefully each of the groups that meet to discuss this material together will include diversity so that more ideas and perspectives can be shared.

In her book *White Fragility*, a must-read for every white person, author and diversity trainer Robin DiAngelo addresses how one of the biggest problems in untangling the insidious roots of racism is how much denial, avoidance, and fragility exists in white folks. For most white people, DiAngelo writes,

> The smallest amount of racial stress is intolerable—the mere suggestion that being white has meaning often triggers a range of defensive responses. These include emotions such as anger, fear, and guilt and behaviors such as argumentation, silence, and withdrawal from the stress-inducing situation.[5]

Do you feel it even now, that pit in your stomach, that clench of resistance?

I always do.

However, we can't talk about the practice of equality without talking about race. In order to do that, we need to recognize our tendencies toward DiAngelo's powerful and telling term that I have come to embrace and observe in myself and so many others in conversation—*white fragility*. Our negative, fragile responses to these conversations, according to DiAngelo, "work to reinstate white equilibrium as they repel the challenge, return our racial comfort, and maintain our dominance within the racial hierarchy."[6]

Our resistance to do the work is telling, and we must accept the challenge, sit in our racial discomfort, and start dismantling our damaging dominance within the racial hierarchy.

I've heard many of my black, brown, and LGBTQ+ activist friends state that white liberal progressives are some of the most difficult voices in the movement toward greater equality. Because a lot of us have taken a few classes or read a few books on race and privilege, we often think we're more "woke" than we really are. I have often prided myself on being a strong advocate for women's and LGBTQ+ and racial equality, especially because my husband is from El Salvador and our five children are brown. In these past few years, however, any measure of pride has been shattered as I've realized I've barely scratched the surface. When our eyes are opened and our hearts stirred, a whole new world opens up and it's filled with unknown territory.

My friend Jennifer Jepsen pastors an open and affirming church plant in Longmont, Colorado. A suburban mom turned social justice activist, she led an examining race and privilege group at The Refuge that gathered people from the wider local community across faiths, ages, and experiences to look hard at racism and privilege. Her eyes initially opened after watching *12 Years a Slave*, a 2013 film based upon Solomon Northup's 1853 memoir of moving from being a free black man in Virginia to twelve years of being enslaved. Her soul was rocked through the film, but it was the death of Michael Brown in Ferguson, Missouri, that was the biggest turning point for her. It helped her identify her "lens of whiteness" for the first time more clearly. To her, the *lens of whiteness* is "a convenient lens that declares that all people have the same start in life, the same opportunity available to them and their children, and disparaging and ignorant terms like 'if they would just. . . .'" Once her lens shifted to a more honest one, she began to recognize white privilege, the lie of white supremacy, and the benefits convened to her through generations of whiteness. Since then, she says, "Everything has now been called into question—every system, every benefit, every comfort, every dream—everything."

A core part of equalizing is that we each honestly own the lie of white supremacy. Stop avoiding it. Stop minimizing it. Stop pretending we're more evolved than we are and just own it.

With the racial divides becoming more apparent in the past few volatile elections not only in the United States but around the world, and the rise of more open white supremacy movements like what happened in Charlottes-ville, Virginia, in 2017, more people are engaging in con-versations about how to examine our race and privilege and practice a better way together. Equalizing won't come through only talking about it, but we can't begin to change things that we haven't properly acknowledged. It makes me think of this passage in Jeremiah 6:14: "You can't heal a wound by saying it's not there!" (TLB)

You can't heal a wound by saying it's not there.

The lie of white supremacy is a festering, deep, and gap-ing wound underneath our church and nation's history.

Get Schooled on the Doctrine of Discovery

As I mentioned in chapter 2, The Refuge hosted an after-noon of learning with Mark Charles, a Navajo writer, prophet, and activist whose voice has been transformative for many people who are open to hearing these difficult truths. In our time together, he systematically challenged the majority of what we'd been taught in school and pro-phetically spoke about the inextricably tangled relation-ship between the church and world history. At the center of his teaching is unpacking the damage the Doctrine of Discovery continues to wreak on the cellular level in our Western white culture.

If you haven't heard of it before, the Doctrine of Dis-covery originated from a series of papal bulls, one of which was issued by Pope Nicholas V in 1452 that states:

[I]nvade, search out, capture, vanquish, and subdue all Saracens and pagans whatsoever, and other ene-mies of Christ wheresoever placed, and the kingdoms, dukedoms, principalities, dominions, possessions, and all movable and immovable goods whatsoever held and possessed by them and to reduce their per-sons to perpetual slavery, and to apply and appro-priate to himself and his successors the kingdoms, dukedoms, counties, principalities, dominions, possessions, and goods, and to convert them to his and their use and profit."[7]

Basically: if they are not already taken by European Christian kingdoms, then go get them, rule them all, wipe them out, steal their stuff, enslave them, take all their lands and hold them to be lesser, forever, in all ways. And, yes, in the name of Christ.

In this book on practice, why an obscure document that most people don't know about? Because over 500 years later, the collateral damage of the Doctrine of Discovery is embedded in our systems—and therefore in us—and we are all still replicating its damage. The United States Declaration of Independence and Constitution, which Americans hold up as our two most formative documents as a nation, fail to acknowledge that they were written entirely by white male colonizers for the benefit of white landowning men. If you live in a different country, you, too, have the Doctrine of Discovery embedded in your story because church and world history are inextricably tied together. Churches served as willing accomplices in the dehumanizing project of settler colonialism.

This is why one of the most tangible practices we can engage with related to equality is to school ourselves in a more honest history and remember that "We the People" in the U.S. Constitution never included all the people. It's rough. It hurts. We will want to find our way to squirm out of our discomfort but it's the work that needs to be done. Read Mark's book that he wrote with Soong-Chan Rah—*Unsettling Truths: The Ongoing, Dehumanizing Legacy of the Doctrine of Discovery*—and let yourself be rocked.

Last year I went to North Carolina and facilitated a shared liturgy at a Confederate monument in the town where my friend Anthony Smith pastors an active missional community. People from different faiths participated. As I watched Anthony, a charismatic black prophet and pastor, and his friend Jim, who is a much more stoic retired white pastor, walk alongside each other around the monument as we prayed, I knew I was standing on holy ground. Denouncing what the monument represents together was a first for their town. Next up for their community: finding a way to remove it. In Denver, one of our public schools recently did the arduous work of changing their name because it honored a former mayor who was an outwardly vocal leader of the Ku Klux Klan in our city years ago.

Our comfortable false mythologies about *who we are* need to be ruined, destroyed, dismantled, and shattered in order for something new and better to be built.

Mutuality Comes from Equality

A long while ago, a popular white Midwestern Christian seminary professor and author wrote a thoughtful response to something I had written about women's equality in church leadership and said he'd like to hear more about *mutuality* and not just *equality*.

I responded, "Me, too, but let's consider a few things first. . . ." Mutuality is one of my highest values and deepest needs; it means mutual dependence, reciprocity. I believe mutuality is the fullest expression of the kingdom of God, with no one over or under another but rather alongside, mutually submitting to one another, sacrificing for each other, following and leading, honoring the giftedness and wisdom of each other, bringing uniqueness to the relationship, giving and receiving, humility and respect.

However, without equality, the expectation of mutuality is imbalanced. It's not right that someone (or a group of people) who holds the most power expects the other person (or group of people) without as much power to submit and play by their rules; yet, this is what groups in power consistently expect. They also usually criticize underrepresented voices for our anger, dissension, and advocating for a better way.

Saying we're equal and *being* equal are two entirely different things. I know this far too well as a woman in leadership amid patriarchal conversations. People of color, the LGBTQ+ community, and many others on the underside of imbalanced power systems know this feeling much more strongly.

Here is a simple truth that the practice of equalizing must include: Equality cannot be defined by how the people who hold the power feel about it.

Equality cannot be defined by how the people who hold the power feel about it.

Recently, The Refuge hosted a workshop called Toxic Masculinity, facilitated by Regan Byrd, an anti-oppression trainer in Denver. Her work is centered on helping us reckon with the corrosive roots of patriarchy and male-dominated culture that are harming all of us. She doesn't water down her message or hold everyone's hands to make people feel better. Let's also be clear—we are not talking about male bashing here. That is not productive or helpful to anyone. Regan is a professional trainer committed to helping people of all ages and experiences change for the better. The brave men who attended have my utmost respect because they came to try to learn. However, let's be honest about these types of experiences—there were a lot more women at the workshop than men. It happens every time and is a core part of the problem. Those with the most power are often missing at these tables of learning. They rarely mutually submit, yet people on the underside of power always are being asked to (and also usually come to learn).

Working for equality will be a rocky road, often feeling divisive. Those on the topside of power, typically those with white, male, economic, straight, and/or religious privilege will be aggravated with the way those on the underside of power often respond. Have you ever wondered or thought or said the following out loud? *Why are they so angry? Why can't they just . . . ? We are doing the best we can, why is it never enough? It's not fair anymore; now they've got all the rights. We're tired of walking on eggshells!*

I get it. I confess I've also felt it. But these are statements from the privileged and powerful, and deepened mutuality can only come from the foundation of truer equality.

Beyond Learning and Lamenting, How Can We Help Equalize?

Beyond studying, learning, breaking out of denial, and fierce and painful self- and systems-examination, there are some concrete ways we can engage in the practice of equalizing in our various unique contexts. Please remember that while this chapter focuses a lot on race and gender, there are many others on the underside of imbalanced power—under-resourced folks, LGBTQ+ persons, those with physical and mental disabilities, the elderly, and religious minorities.

As you read through this list of possibilities to equalize in our different contexts, notice internally: Which of these make you extra nervous or a little scared to try? Which are you drawn to and know you need courage to practice? Which do you want to engage with as a next step?

We're all different, but hopefully our commonality is that we won't just talk about equality but will actually play our brave part—no matter how big or small—in being equalizers.

Ways We Can Equalize:

— *Open our eyes and start noticing.* We have to break out of denial and begin to see almost everything through a new lens. Start to notice homogeneous leadership and groups. See who's got the power, microphone, and voices of authority, and notice ratios of men and women, people of color, binary and nonbinary folks in every system we are in.

— *Make new friends.* Forge new friendships, nurture spaces and places where we can listen, learn, eat, love, grow alongside people not like us. Bravely nurture cross-gender, cross-culture, and multiracial friendships.

— *Examine whom we need to listen to and learn from.* If we're white, we can never know what it's like to be a person of color. We can only listen and learn from our friends who are. The same goes for those who come from a different gender identity, socioeconomic demographic, with mental and physical disabilities, or culture or faith different from ours. *Who do you need to listen to? What groups are on your heart, and how can you engage in listening to their stories, realities, passions, and truth?*

— *Invite new leaders to the table.* When forming groups and teams, ask first, who else can we invite to join us to create a more balanced team? If you don't know, ask someone with less power who does.

— *Fan new voices into flame.* Inviting to the table is only a first step; actually drawing out and hearing untapped, under-supported voices always needs intention. Ask for opinions (and brace ourselves for harsh but much-needed truth). Consider going around the room to get everyone's input instead of letting the dominant voices control out of habit and privilege. Then, take the time to go around a second (or third) time to get input from the people who didn't feel comfortable speaking the first round.

— *Vote with our feet and money.* Refuse to be part of unequal systems, period. One of the reasons inequality is perpetuated is that those with privilege and power refuse to break the status quo. To practice equality, we will need to vote with our feet and money and not slink away but be honest about why we can't support systems that refuse to acknowledge their power imbalance and unhealthiness.

— *Take the heat for change.* Justice is costly, but we need more courageous people from all ages and experiences who refuse to buckle under pressure and hold the line on core issues of greater equality.

— *Ask for help.* Part of what gets us stuck sometimes is we aren't sure what to do or how to do it and remain paralyzed. Ask others we know who are advocates and allies and learn from them.

It's also crucial to add that we will have to pay a cost for the practice of equalizing. Part of justice is taking a hit for these values. Our boat rocking will sometimes cause others to jump ship. If we are leaders in ministry or business, we could lose our jobs. If we have sexist and racist family members, our new awareness may cause a great disruption in our relationships. The more we change, the more others around us who aren't shifting in the same way often become uncomfortable.

I know many pastors and leaders who have lost their positions over issues of equality. When they began to talk about it in their congregations or move to put particular unrepresented people into leadership positions or do the hard work of moving toward full LGBTQ+ equality or begin to have frank conversations about immigrants and white privilege, some donors get uncomfortable. And those donors keep our systems afloat. Brave leadership will be needed to absorb the cost of doing the right thing on behalf of change and living with the loss of money, people, our former reputations.

The fascinating part is that this crosses faith expressions, too. At my multifaith group, I have talked to clergy from Buddhist, Jewish, and Unitarian Universalist congregations, and each of them say the same thing—these kinds of frank and soul-disrupting conversations about race and privilege in their communities always create anxiety. Still, these courageous leaders are committed to shaking up their people and paying the cost of equality.

The Road to Equality Is Paved with Friendship

To summarize the practice of equalizing into one chapter is not an easy task, and there's far more to flesh out in the challenging work of being equalizers. The Dig Deeper list at the end of this chapter offers book ideas to engage more intentionally. However, conversations on equalizing wouldn't be complete without remembering the road to equality is paved with friendship.

Friendship and connections to real stories, real lives, changes everything.

Until I knew my unhoused neighbors as friends, I believed their reality was somehow their fault. Until I listened to the painful stories of my black brothers and sisters and their daily experiences, I stayed in comfortable denial. Until I broke bread with my friends with mental illness and ravaging addictions and heard their hearts, I thought there were simple solutions to their realities. Until I sat with my LGBTQ+ friends in the dark as they came out and started walking toward freedom, I espoused a theology that deeply harmed.

Friendship, equality, and practice are all mixed up together.

Friendship is what will break down walls and build new bridges and pave the way for real equality. When across our differences we learn how to be friends, everything changes. Power shifts, healing happens, freedom comes, and we taste a bit of heaven on earth, here and now. Friendship equalizes.

While I was working on this chapter, fifty Muslims were violently murdered in Christchurch, New Zealand, during Friday prayers at two mosques. The devastation of yet another hate crime waged by white supremacists rocked the world and magnified so many people's desires to be more engaged in real relationship with others who aren't like us. One of my closest friends is mentoring a young refugee from a Muslim country, and they are forging a new and beautiful friendship across cultural differences. Now, Islamophobia isn't some distant concept from the news; it's something Marty's friend is experiencing here, now. Because of their relationship, Marty is more protective, active, and brave on behalf of the Muslim community than when she didn't know anyone in real life. Her life is being forever changed by the simple act of friendship.

Despite our best intentions, equalizing will never be mastered and will always be one of the most difficult practices for humans. We will often feel tired, discouraged, angry, embarrassed, and completely overwhelmed with ourselves and others along the way. We won't see the results we long for and will see parts of people and systems that we wish we could un-see.

But we won't relent.
We can't relent.
Equality will never drop out of the sky, so we're all the
    world's got.

As we end this chapter, take a few minutes to take a deep breath and take in the magnitude of these last two practices. They are heavy, intense. Including and equalizing will not come in a rush; these practices are lifetime work and embracing the long story of transformation is helpful for lasting over the long haul. We must also always remember our humanity in each of these practices. Nothing in this book is able to be fully mastered. There's no way to get an A+ (for all you overachievers) or to fail (for all you who are used to barely passing). None of these ideas are simple or formulaic. However, the purpose of this book is to stir us to be the change we want to see in the world, live out faith as a verb, embody something different, and move toward progress not perfection.

Next is the practice of advocating, a way we can evoke creative, tangible change in our own lives, others' lives, and the world. There's a lot of work to be done. As author Craig Greenfield wrote in *Subversive Jesus: An Adventure in Justice, Mercy, and Faithfulness in a Broken World*: "I have found that if I pray for God to move a mountain, I must be prepared to wake up next to a shovel."[8]

Grab your shovel. There's a lot more work to do.

A PRAYER FOR EQUALIZING

God, we confess we've benefitted from systems that oppress.
We lament the imbalance and inequality that's been perpetuated as normal.
Help us boldly act to break down barriers to equality.
May we play our part in equalizing in tangible ways that restore, reconcile, and renew.
Amen.

FOR PERSONAL REFLECTION

1. Consider the images of *over* and *under* one another. Can you see some of the groups and systems you've been part of and how you've been over others, somehow better than them? Who? How have you been under others? What has that looked like, felt like?
2. Reflect on your own privilege. What do you carry without even thinking about it that you need to acknowledge more fully and honestly?

3. Review the list of ways to practice equalizing. Which are the most challenging for you?
4. How you have seen friendship equalize, either in your own life or in another example? Reflect on how real relationship changes our perspectives.

FOR GROUP REFLECTION

1. Share with the group what challenged you most about this chapter. What was the most encouraging?
2. Reflect on the image that depicts the difference between false equality and creative justice and the need for more imaginative solutions to ensure equality for all. What resonates?
3. If you are white, how are you trying to own and acknowledge the lie of white supremacy?
4. Read the excerpt from the Doctrine of Discovery out loud together. What words did you notice? What does reading it stir up in you?
5. What do you think about the idea of equality preceding mutuality?
6. Review the "Ways We Can Equalize" section. Which do you resonate with? What are some contexts you can apply them in?

TO PRACTICE

1. Consider the list of different ways to practice equalizing. Choose one that you are being challenged to try and do it in your particular context.
2. If you are in a leadership position of any kind, use your position to create tools, skills, learning on

disparate power centered on race, gender, sexuality. Organize a workshop, training, conversation and reflect on the resistance and learning that happens there.

3. Because part of the practice of equalizing begins with self-reflection and honest lament, commit to read some of the resources provided in the Dig Deeper section below. If you can, find someone who wants to read along with you so you can process it together.

4. Lose something because of your dedication to equality. Pay a cost, take a hit, risk disapproval, do what you know is right.

5. Intentionally nurture a friendship with someone who is typically on the underside of power. Listen and learn from their story.

6. Attend an anti-racism or anti-oppression workshop or class in your local community and submit yourself to learning.

DIG DEEPER

Better: Waking Up to Who We Could Be by Melvin Bray

Jesus Feminist: God's Radical Notion That Women Are People Too by Sarah Bessey

I'm Still Here: Black Dignity in a World Made for Whiteness by Austin Channing Brown

Unsettling Truths: The Ongoing, Dehumanizing Legacy of the Doctrine of Discovery by Mark Charles and Soong-Chan Rah

White Fragility: Why It's So Hard for White People to Talk about Racism by Robin DiAngelo

White Rage: The Unspoken Truth of Our Racial Divide by Carol Anderson

CHAPTER 6

___

THE PRACTICE OF
ADVOCATING

Ad·vo·cate — *ad-vuh-keyt*
Verb / present participle: **advocating**
1. To work on behalf of someone in need of justice, support, or care
2. To empower and hold others up

*People say, what is the sense of our small effort? They
cannot see that we must lay one brick at a time, take one
step at a time. A pebble cast into a pond causes ripples that
spread in all directions.*

—Dorothy Day[1]

My husband — Jose — is a pro bono lawyer for Spanish-
speaking domestic violence victims; he's also a pilot and
a lieutenant colonel in the Army. Yes, he's a real under-
achiever! He's also one of the best advocates I know. He
boldly advocates for those who — for a variety of reasons —
need someone alongside them to help them find healing,
hope, and change after messy domestic abuse. I rarely get

to see him in action in court, but when I do, I am over-come with emotion. At a custody court appearance for a struggling friend, I watched him advocate; my soul stirred and my desire to keep advocating for others magnified. As I heard him fiercely and tenderly represent his client, I thought to myself: "This is what it looks like to have an advocate, to have someone fight for you, to empower someone to share their story and tell their truth."

It is fitting that in Spanish, the word for lawyer is *abogado*—advocate. But what is an advocate beyond a professional lawyer? When I asked our group of Refuge advocates what some other words for "advocate" are, here's what they shared: someone who comes alongside someone else, supporter, encourager, helper, friend, coach, strengthener, a soundboard, a help-figure-it-out-er, challenger, defender, listener, cheerleader, someone who helps uncover our voice.

In the Christian Scriptures, the Greek word for "advo-cate" is *paraklētos*. *Para* means "alongside" and *kletos* is "called in aid." In John 14:16–18, it is used to describe the Holy Spirit and means "summoned, called to one's side or aid." It also means: comforter, helper, aid, assis-tant, encourager. I consider advocating to mean encourag-ing, strengthening, coming alongside, giving voice to the silenced, defending, and using our voice, power, and influ-ence on behalf of change.

A core principle in our Refuge group is that we all can *be* an advocate and we all *need* an advocate. They are not mutually exclusive. Often, we have a tendency as helpers to want to help others but not want help for ourselves. It makes me think of Jesus' example in John 13 in the upper room before his betrayal, arrest, and crucifixion and why washing his disciples' feet despite their initial resistance is so profound. Washing other people's feet isn't hard for a lot of us; we like to get our hands dirty, to feel useful, helpful, caring. But to have others' hands touch our dirty feet? No way, that's way too vulnerable!

When I ask people, "Would you rather give or receive?" the response is 100 percent consistent: Hands down, everyone likes giving far better. That's because it's much easier. When we're talking about practicing, *easy* is usually an indicator that we're not engaged at a transformative level. It's not a sign of doing something wrong, but it does point to the possibility we're not allowing ourselves to be immersed in the practice, instead remaining safely on the sidelines of our heart and experience. Again, a core Refuge value is that "everyone gives, everyone receives."

That's how true advocacy works.

My friend Melanie Dewey, codirector of Mercy Ministries with Diane Pulvermiller, has been working with orphans in Romania for several decades. The Roma, long pejoratively called *gypsies*, are the underclass in Romanian culture, an oppressed and ostracized group that does not have equal access to resources and are consistently the most impoverished in their country. Melanie and her husband, Scott, adopted a son as he aged out of the system and have been fierce advocates for him from across the globe (he was recently the victim of our oppressive immigration laws and remains in Romania)—at great expense both emotionally and financially. Watching them care for their son has been incredibly inspiring because none of it makes "sense" from a middle-class, sensible mindset. Yet, he is a child of God, worthy of dignity, respect, and someone to fight for him. They do all they can to remind him and others of that.

Melanie shares how so often these kids are viewed through a lens of *worthy* or *not worthy*. She says, "Those who are compliant are deemed worthy of help. Those who make waves are not." I have found this to be so true! If people submit themselves to helpers the way helpers feel comfortable with, then all is well. If not, they are considered ungrateful, rebellious, or lazy. Melanie adds, "We have run into so many 'helpers' who refuse to understand the effects of early childhood trauma on our young people." They expect them to behave a certain way instead of doing what Melanie says is most desperately needed, to provide "safe relationships with people who will love them no matter what, so the kids can begin to learn more healthy ways of keeping themselves safe and connected to others." Melanie and Scott are not American saviors. They are fellow strugglers, deeply dedicated to walking alongside others, offering healing and dignity where it's been lost. To last this long, they've needed passionate advocates for themselves—friends, allies, supporters who recognize their realities and encourage them to keep *not making sense*. They embody "with."

The Difference between *to*, *for*, and *with*

Many years ago I participated in a conversation hosted by a Tacoma nonprofit organization called Street Psalms. Joined with other grassroots pastors and leaders dedicated to being people of presence in hard places, we processed the power of prepositions. The language of *with*, as opposed to *to* and *for*, changes everything.

Here's the difference:

The preposition *to* is paternal and creates oppression.
The preposition *for* is maternal and creates codependence.
The preposition *with* is incarnational and creates transformation.

I've written and spoken extensively on these three prepositions over the years, and the differences between them are core to the conversation on advocacy. The prepositions *to* and *for* come easiest to humans, especially if we were raised in church or involved in missions-oriented projects. *To* is paternal; it is built on principle that we are somehow better than others, have something to give *to them* or some wisdom or help to impart. The problem with *to* is that it becomes a posture of power that is patronizing, disempowering, and implies *I'm somehow above you* (similar to being *over* others from the practice of equalizing chapter we engaged with right before this one). It often makes the one on the receiving end feel like a project or less-than and is not at all reciprocal.

The preposition *for* is another easy reflex for most of us and the one that is most easy for me as a mother of five, Enneagram 2 (helper) style, adult child of an alcoholic, and a tried-and-true nurturer. The style of the preposition *for* is maternal and is centered on us wanting to do things *for* others. Much of the preposition *for* is centered on us taking care of others so that our anxiety is relieved: "Let me fix this for you, take care of this for you, do this for you." *For*, in many faith circles and caring professions, is highly valued. In conversations on being more like Jesus, caring for the poor and marginalized, and engaging in real life with people, it's also most common. The problem with *for* is that it creates codependence, which is an unhealthy relationship where helpers get sucked into helping, make things happen for others, or remain in control through helping. Both *to* and *for* are one-way, one-up/one-down relationships.

In the practice of advocating, we need to notice our tendency to want to default to *to* and *for*. They're far easier than the messy, beautiful work of *with*.

The preposition *with* is core to healthy advocacy. *With* is incarnational, in the flesh, heart to heart, shoulder to shoulder, eye to eye. It is built on equal value, mutuality, and arises from relationship instead of stepping in and trying to solve problems on our own terms. *With* is centered on "I am with you, not walking ahead but alongside." "I want to learn from you, too" and "We're here, together." *With* breaks down imbalanced power from the relationship and recognizes the fundamental dignity of the person and begins with listening for the deeper story that informs the suffering.

One of the biggest dangers for us helper and controlling types is our desire to be an advocate on our terms, in our way, and often without people's permission. This is not an advocate; that's just an annoying boundary breaker. Advocacy stems from relationship, from a desire on both sides to be connected, from the core value of *with*.

I can't tell you the number of times people have told me they are tired of being people's projects. It gets old. My friend Tami has had countless people try to help her with her mental and physical struggles through the years but few people who want to be in reciprocal relationship with her. Her words one day in a phone call have echoed in my heart for years: "I don't want someone to try to fix me. I just need a friend."

Magnifying Voices

My friend Suzann Mollner is the executive director of Beirut and Beyond, a nonprofit organization dedicated to reconciliation, relief, and relationship on behalf of Palestinian refugees. She's been in the trenches as an advocate and ally for going on two decades; after all these years, the work hasn't become easier. When we maintain a safe and comfortable distance from people in *to* and *for* relationships, there's not much of a cost. Suzann is one of the best examples of *with* I have ever witnessed. It's also why she's sometimes truly undone by the cruelties being handed down to her friends by an oppressive system that continues to perpetuate more damage and less relief, year after year.

With bright green eyes and impassioned words on behalf of her friends, Suzann shares the hardest part about being an advocate is the mistrust people feel toward the people she cares the most about. Islamophobia is rampant, and the stories she shares from the depths of her heart are often met with fearful comments, misinformation, and ambivalence. It's worn her down over the years, but she believes, "If someone is silenced, I am silenced. I am not free until we are all free, and that includes Palestinians, too."

Because the majority of Palestinians are consigned to camps throughout the Middle East, the real voices of the struggling men, women, and children are often not heard, other than the loud exceptions that often make our news reports and are always related to bombings and violence. A central part of advocacy is magnifying voices that are often unheard. Suzann's whole life is dedicated to this. When I visited a refugee camp in the West Bank several years ago for the first time, I asked the speaker—who had lived in the camp for sixty years after his entire family was removed from their home in Jaffa—what we could do to support them from afar? Amar's response: "Tell our story."

Tell our story.

His chance of getting their story into the ears and hearts of people with power are slim to none. However, as an advocate and ally, we can use our power and privilege on behalf of this simple task. *Just tell our story.* Tell what we experienced, witnessed, learned. I've been doing it ever since (often with predictable resistance because of the false narrative that's been perpetuated about Palestinians). But I won't stop sharing it. Each time a bit of Amar's voice is heard.

Advocates tell stories.

When considering advocacy for people around the world who need support, we often hear the Christian phrase, "We need to be a voice for the voiceless." There's no passage in the Bible specifically about being a voice *for* the voiceless; that's terminology we adopted. However, when considering our responsibility to help advocate on behalf of those whose voices are silenced, I love the words of the prophet Isaiah in the Old Testament, or Hebrew Bible. It's our responsibility to "learn to do good; seek justice, rescue the oppressed, defend the orphan . . ." (v. 1:17). Later, in chapter 58, it says,

"Is not this the kind of fasting I have chosen:
to loose the chains of injustice
    and untie the cords of the yoke,

to set the oppressed free
and break every yoke?
Is it not to share your food with the hungry
and to provide the poor
wanderer with shelter —
when you see the naked, to clothe them,
and not to turn away from your own flesh and blood?"

Isaiah 58:6–7 NIV

Everyone has a voice. Our role as advocates is to magnify it.

We are called to advocate on behalf of those whose voices have been silenced by life experiences, systemic oppression, generational poverty, and a myriad of other things that squelch God's image.

One of my favorite Jesus stories centered on advocating is an unlikely one, in John 8. Jesus stands between the woman accused of adultery and those about to stone her to death and advocates on her behalf in his typical subtle, creative way. Had he not advocated for her, she would have died. In her situation, even if she had tried to use her voice, it wouldn't have mattered. No one would have listened. *Everything in the system was completely stacked against her.* She needed someone with power to stand and speak on her behalf.

A virgin sold into a brothel in India can't speak for herself. Her only hope is an advocate who will fight for justice on her behalf. A man with a mental disability can't open certain doors in the system to get the resources he needs without an advocate's help no matter how much we'd like to believe he could on his own. A person who lives outside can't cross certain practical bridges without someone moving some of the real and strong obstacles out of the way first. An orphan in an orphanage can't magically find their way into a family. A kid being bullied usually can't defend themselves alone without paying a huge cost. A woman who deeply desires to break into leadership in a system that doesn't actively honor her gifts will never be granted a seat at that table without someone with power actively advocating for her presence. A person who has been sexually abused won't automatically have the confidence, strength, and security they need to stand strong in tricky situations. An undocumented immigrant can't show up in certain moments to plead their case because the risk of unwarranted detention is too great.

Advocates come alongside and support those who can't say it themselves.

I met my friend Sarah Jackson when she was renting a one-bedroom apartment across from the Immigration Detention Center in Denver and decided to open up her apartment to let families visiting detainees sleep in her bed while she took the couch. In her mid-twenties with long black hair and a sharp wit, Sarah gives me hope for the future. Many years later, her little apartment has now evolved into a beautiful thriving advocacy and hospitality house called Casa de Paz—House of Peace—where she and her team of volunteers are doing what she did from the beginning—offer support and hospitality freely to immigration detention detainees and their families. These people are often detained not only for months but for years, separated from their families, with none of the rights that are afforded by our U.S. judicial system. Without advocates like Sarah and other tireless immigration activists, their voices are completely silenced. I have watched Sarah tell stories online for many years now, speak at multiple churches and organizations, and do whatever she can to raise awareness on the realities of immigration detainees in our city. She embodies the practice of advocating on a public level, but we all can play, too. What stories can we tell? How can we use our privilege, power, and resources to elevate the voices of those who can't say it themselves?

In order to do this we can't remain distant, protected, or comfortable. We'll have to be engaged in real relationship together. I am reminded of the words of Peruvian theologian and champion for the poor, Gustavo Gutiérrez: "You say you care about the poor? Tell me their names."[2]

Ordinary Activism

Every movement toward change has required passionate advocates who pushed against the system to invoke change. Without the suffragettes, women wouldn't have earned the right to vote; even then it took fifty more years before women of color could vote more freely (and even today there are still significant barriers to that). However, without the civil rights movement and many lives lost through it, we'd still have segregated drinking fountains and separate seats on buses. Groups of people banding together, using our voices and feet and votes on behalf of unjust laws, is one of the most powerful forms of advocacy. There is something extremely transformational about a shared passion despite our differences and putting our boots to the ground to enact change. I have many friends who have been arrested for their advocacy against capital punishment, mass incarceration, and cruel and discriminatory police tactics. Many community organizers dedicate their entire lives to actions that inspire systemic change, and I have deep respect for their sacrifice.

But what about the average high school student, suburban mom, or blue-collar worker? What about the uneducated, the ones without gas or a smart phone with nifty apps that automatically faxes letters to legislators? What about ordinary people who have never participated in civil engagement before and aren't quite sure if their voice makes a difference? Where does activism fit in for us? The answer is everywhere!

On social movements, everyone can play and be an advocate.

The biggest questions for all of us remain the same: What's our part? What can I do? What is challenging for me but still possible given my unique circumstance? A lot of us have images in our head of what activism is supposed to look like — a particular brand of protestor, someone who shows up at every event with a sign, or a person who is extremely well-versed in every aspect of certain political and social issues.

I love the embodiment of ordinary activists where we all can play our part in advocating for change.

Some of the ways we can advocate is through writing letters, making phone calls, showing up at city or county meetings and town halls, speaking with legislators and influencers, signing petitions, and learning more about particular issues so we can be more educated on not only how we vote but also how we communicate with others about core issues that matter.

After the 2016 election in the United States, I started a monthly advocacy group at our house called Use Your Voice. We gathered for a few hours once a month to share issues and actions and gain some traction on getting calls and letters done for the areas we were most passionate about. None of us had to align our views perfectly or do or say things a certain way. A strange mix of old and young, married and single, resourced and non-resourced, we were as *ordinary* as we could possibly be. Yet, there was something strangely powerful about our individual voices being used as part of a collective one in an intentional and creative way. One of the highlights of our work was to write handwritten thank-you notes to people who were in the trenches advocating, legislating, and helping fight for change. Many of these folks are rarely thanked, and the simple act of writing them a thank-you note was a way we advocated for the advocates. Our group no longer meets in person but we still share ideas on our group page and it continues to inspire us to keep using our voice however we can on behalf of others.

Holly Roach Knight is a dear friend and faith-rooted community organizer in Asheville, North Carolina. White, married, and passionate about social change, she uses her privilege on behalf of others, helping people consider ways they can advocate for change in their context. Ordinary activism, she says, has to do with "ordinary people understanding they are part of how change happens and how the world gets to be a better place. Ordinary activism erupts from people's hearts and guts; they see an injustice, know that harm is being done, and step in to do something about it."

Heroic acts aren't just about running into a burning building to save someone. It's also rising up and saying, "No, I will not let my brothers and sisters be treated this way or the community that I live in harm the vulnerable." The vulnerable are not only people; it's our planet as well.

Holly also studies systems change, and recently shared with me how one of the primary ways justice movements get stuck is by fostering exclusivity. She adds, "Our movement culture has set a high bar for admission that doesn't reflect the welcome and love it is supposed to be fostering." It's not that the professionals aren't sometimes needed to help lead and guide social actions, but without a fluidity and openness to all levels of participation—including the very ordinary human beings who care—it will become elitist, closed, and not do what it's intended to do: *build greater health in our communities.*

"I Did It Myself!"

Taking things to a more microlevel, we can also help people practice better self-advocacy. At The Refuge, we often say: "Friends don't go hard places alone." When going to particular appointments or meetings at certain agencies, many people often aren't treated well, are given confusing instructions, and end up feeling disempowered. What we can do as part of the practice of advocacy is sit alongside while our friends practice using their voice; we are available to clarify things and to be a translator of some sort if necessary. I don't come in and take over (even though my *for* tendencies definitely want to kick in) but rather try to remain a cheerleader and encourager. In the same vein, advocates also help the person in authority know they can't dismiss, mistreat, or neglect my friends.

Over the years, I have watched the incredible difference it makes when an advocate is present in the conversation, not to speak for people but to get the attention of those who have often ignored them, build bridges of dignity, and break down barriers together.

Years ago, I helped my long-time friend Cindy apply for disability. It was an arduous process, and I was reminded how tilted our system is against people who are under-resourced or lack certain physical and mental abilities. Single, white, and now in her sixties, with a high school education, many would think, Why can't she just get it done? Here's why: the paperwork, the process, is so freaking complicated that even the most educated, skilled, and resourced person hits multiple obstacles that make us want to give up. I have a master's degree and years of experience advocating, yet often when I read some of her paperwork I am equally confused.

Journeying alongside Cindy for many years, I have learned how desperately we need an army of advocates in almost every context. Together with many other amazing Refuge friends, we have all learned better advocacy skills walking alongside Cindy. I have sat next to her while she made a phone call to try to get her dental bill reduced and heard the person on the other end of the phone say, "No, sorry, we definitely can't help you." Then, I got on the phone, explained I'm her advocate, and in a few short minutes she had a large reduction in her bill and a payment plan she can afford. It sometimes makes me feel sick and also is an example of how sometimes doing things *for* people is necessary because of our broken systems. Regardless, it's also a strong reminder of why the practice of advocating is critically important and how without people to come alongside and break down the obstacles, many will continue to suffer a wide array of consequences alone.

However, healthy advocacy isn't only to help open doors for others, it's also helping inspire people to practice for themselves.

Cindy is honest and has said that she wishes we'd always make her calls for her; it would be far easier that way. However, that's not transformational. Slowly, surely, I have watched her begin to advocate for herself more tangibly, even when it's hard. She's picked up the phone on her own, made appointments, followed through. Years ago, she couldn't do it but after a lot of modeling and encouraging, she's starting to advocate for herself much more consistently. A few months ago, after a stroke that has been another blow to her mobility, she was really proud of some steps she took to arrange rides on her own—something that a while back she wouldn't have the strength to do. She exclaimed, "Yep, I did it myself! See, I'm learning!"

I was thrilled but also reminded—advocating is a long game. It would have been easy to give up on Cindy years ago when she wasn't doing it the way we wanted her to fast enough.

Everything related to advocacy is deeply spiritual. It's a place we grow in patience, trust, love, and healthy boundaries and wrestle with how to manage our anger, irritation, frustration, and despair. Advocacy is a form of solidarity with others. My friend, author and teacher Mark Votava, lives and teaches in South Korea and reminds us,

> Solidarity with others is a big part of manifesting love. This is what it means to become fully alive and deeply human. We lay down our prejudices, biases, opinions, perceptions, and arrogance in order to really see someone else in our common humanity.[3]

Cindy's not a project. She's me, she's you.

Permission Advocates

I like to break rules. Not the kind that say, "Don't feed the animals" or "No trespassing" or "Stand in line and wait your turn." Those, I tend to honor. I'm talking about internal and unspoken rules embedded into the cultures of our structures and systems. Now I like to break those kinds of rules, but I wasn't always that way.

For many years, I played it safe and tried to toe the line in the structures and systems I moved in. I was quieter, more inclined to wait for someone to ask for my opinion instead of offering it freely. I was more apt to go with the flow instead of bringing up counterpoints. I was far more likely to play nice and push down some of my ideas or perspectives because I didn't want to rock the boat. That waiting for the right time, the perfect ask, the stars to align, the (fill in the blank) probably was going to mean I would wait a long time for some things I deeply cared about to come to fruition.

I was stuck with a feeling that some of you might be able to relate to as well —*the need to ask for permission to validate our work, abilities, passion, and gifts.* We are often really skilled at giving our power to others. We assume there is someone above us, better than us, with more skills than us, stronger than us, louder than us, more educated than us, more articulate than us, more spiritual than us who needs to grant us permission to move forward on our contributions, our dreams, our passions. My friend Angie Fadel is a gifted spiritual director and meditative archery coach and writes what she calls "mantras for the rest of us" that help empower women, the LGBTQ+ community, and those who are often undervalued. A recent one said, "My power doesn't come from your approval. It resides in my DNA."

As we wrap up this chapter on the practice of advocating, can you think of something you might be waiting for permission from someone else to do? Is there something in your gut or your heart or your flesh or your bones that is stirring, growing, brewing, longing, moving, developing, birthing, waiting, wondering, hoping? Maybe it's in there, but it's scary and vulnerable to say it. You're afraid of being misunderstood. You know it will ruffle feathers. You have a long list of reasons you're not qualified. Many of us might be waiting for someone to give us permission to do it, but maybe we don't need permission after all. Maybe what we need is a *permission advocate.*

I consider permission advocates safe friends, family, and advocates who will help us quit waiting for permission from outside sources and encourage us to give it to ourselves and move forward on some of our dreams.

Leaving jobs, untangling from abusive relationships, pursuing dreams, returning to school, igniting a passion — I've traveled with countless friends who have found their way to something new when they had a permission advocate in their lives who reminded them they didn't need someone else to approve. Their own personal permission was what mattered. Brené Brown, in her book *Rising Strong*, reminds us, too: "Many of us will spend our entire lives trying to slog through the shame swampland to get to a place where we can give ourselves permission to both be imperfect and to believe we are enough."[4]

Let me be a permission advocate for you right now:

You don't need someone else's permission to do what is stirring in your heart.

Your power doesn't come from someone's approval; it resides in your DNA.

You are enough. You are gloriously imperfect. There's a whole lot of work to be done that can never get done if you keep waiting for permission.

As we wind down this chapter, consider the practice of advocating in your context. What would shifting relationships to *with* instead of *to* and *for* look like? How can you use your voice to magnify others? Is there someone who could use an advocate to feel permission to do something that feels foreign or hard? Do you? There's a commonly shared phrase extrapolated from the Jewish tradition that says, *Every blade of grass has its own angel bending over it, whispering, "Grow, grow."* May we be these kinds of angels for each other.

Healing. Listening. Loving. Including. Equalizing. Advocating. We've covered a lot of ground so far together. As you can tell, each of these practices are intertwined, part of a big pond where the ripples spill into one another. Each of them are in the blood and guts of the human experience. Nothing about them is neat and tidy, and our intersection with ourselves and others is sure to stir up grief. Next we're going to dive into the practice of mourning, an often forgotten one in the age of speed, efficiency, and pain avoidance.

A PRAYER FOR ADVOCATING

God, help us learn what it means to be with others.
Give us patience, perseverance, and humility as we advocate and
  encourage.
Keep us grounded in the ordinary as we magnify voices and use our
  own.
May justice and healing prevail.
Amen.

FOR PERSONAL REFLECTION

1. Who in your life has been an advocate for you? How did it make a difference in your story?
2. When it comes to the prepositions *to, for,* or *with,* which are most natural for you?
3. Are there particular voices you feel called to magnify? Why?
4. Are you needing to give yourself permission to say or do something you're afraid of?

FOR GROUP REFLECTION

1. What are some words that you would use to describe an *advocate?* Brainstorm your own list together.
2. Review the differences between *to, for,* and *with* together. Which is most natural for you? Can you think of some personal examples where you are trying to embody *with?*
3. Engage with the idea of ordinary activism. How are you playing your part in advocating for change? What has it felt like for you?
4. Think of your present circumstances—what's going on in your life right now? How might you need an advocate? Consider these prompts: "I really need help with . . . I feel extremely lonely in . . . I'm trying to figure out. . . ."
5. Is there something you are waiting for permission for instead of doing what is stirring up in your heart? Try sharing it with the group.

TO PRACTICE

1. Notice how often in relationship, to relieve your own anxiety, you give unsolicited advice, share the words "you should," or step in to help others.
2. If you haven't before, show up at a local march, attend a city council meeting, write a letter to a legislator about an issue you care about, or make a phone call that shares your passion.
3. Volunteer in some tangible way at a local non-profit organization that advocates for people seeking support (the unhoused, domestic violence, mental health, LGBTQ+, disabilities, single parents, struggling kids). Begin to listen to the stories, observe trained advocates, and learn more about these important issues.
4. Go with someone to a government agency, or a legal, doctor's, or other hard appointment and just be present alongside them. Notice what you observe about how they are treated, and the complexity of the system.

DIG DEEPER

Beyond Our Efforts: A Celebration of Denver Peacemaking by The Center for Urban Peacemakers

The Irresistible Revolution: Living as an Ordinary Radical by Shane Claiborne

Just Mercy: A Story of Justice and Redemption by Bryan Stevenson

Raise Your Voice: Why We Stay Silent and How to Speak Up by Kathy Khang

Standing at the Edge: Finding Freedom Where Fear and Courage Meet by Joan Halifax

CHAPTER 7

THE PRACTICE OF
MOURNING

Mourn — *mohrn*
Verb / present participle: **mourning**
1. To feel the pain and sadness of grief
2. To experience the heartache of a death or loss
3. To emotionally express feelings of lament

Our tears are sacred.
They water the ground around our feet so that new things can grow.[1]
— Rob Bell

On my son Jamison's twenty-second birthday, my dad —
after four months of home hospice — took his last breath in
my presence. Sitting on the bed next to him, hearing the
rise and fall of his chest get further and further apart, reality
set in. This was really it, his time to "wade in the water" as
he called it. My relationship with my dad, a lifelong alcoholic, was always both tender and painful. During most of
my childhood and early adulthood, I longed for his more
active presence in my life, and part of my healing journey

in my thirties was to reckon with his inability to do that the way I desperately desired. When he received his diagnosis and said yes to our invitation to come live with us in Colorado so we could take care of him in his last days, we were shocked. Usually fiercely independent, in the face of death something shifted; he knew he didn't want to be alone. Every day, for four months, we talked openly about dying. The hospice workers fell in love with him, and my local friends witnessed what a healthy death could look like. It was a thin place, where earth and heaven met and words fell short.

As his breaths got shallower, I whispered, "Daddy, the water's good. You can wade in the water now. You get to go on Jamison's birthday." His last breath a few seconds later was the beginning of a new season of mourning for me. This time it wasn't mourning for the dad I didn't have growing up. Now, it was missing the loss of his infectious laughter, his wild and vivid stories, and his twinkling blue eyes. It was realizing he'd never again comment on my Facebook posts with the same thing he always wrote on every single post—"Luv u CassaBlue" (It makes me cry just writing it).

Grief is weird and comes in waves. The reality of that much intensity in such a short period of time while juggling my twins' last year of high school, Refuge life, and beginning to write this book hits me in the strangest moments.

A few weeks after the one-year anniversary of my dad's death, I received the email that my friend Rachel Held Evans, an author many of you probably read and loved, died at age thirty-seven after a sudden illness. Her death has sparked a collective grief among so many who were deeply moved and inspired by her words, heart, and guts. I am still in shock, disoriented, and profoundly sad. The day after she died, I flew to San Diego for the memorial service for a long-time friend who lost a four-month battle with cancer at the age of fifty-five. Our son dying just a few short months later—the worst possible grief—has rocked us to the depths of our souls. As these tumultuous waves of loss slammed into my soul, I have felt the fragility of being human like never before.

You have likely experienced your own losses and are acquainted with life's fragility, too. You know what it's like to lose someone, something, a hope, a dream, your faith. You get the reality that we can never go back to the way things were. For most of us, the hardest part isn't knowing what loss feels like. We've got that one nailed down. The trickier work is knowing what to do with our loss and how to mourn.

Now what?

There are many different forms, but to me, mourning is *allowing ourselves to feel hurt, sorrow, anger, loss, and grief.* In the second beatitude in the Sermon on the Mount, Jesus says it's a blessing to mourn, and we will be comforted. In the Jewish tradition, part of the rituals for death include sitting shivah, a week-long ritual of visitation and public grief, then shloshim until the thirty-day mark, or the one-year anniversary for the loss of a parent. Native American tribes have diverse ways of honoring their dead that are tangible and creative. Years ago when I visited the Pine Ridge reservation in South Dakota, one of the women I met was preparing for the one-year anniversary of her son's death. The ritual was a big party where all the stops were pulled out with gifts and a feast for everyone even though she had little to no money. The planned celebration didn't minimize her pain. Rather, it honored it. Public spaces for grief give room for what needs to be said: "I see you, pain."

Less than a week after Jared died, we had a celebration of life at The Refuge, our beloved faith community. We experienced the power of deep collective grief and shared hope. It was the most raw, vulnerable, and healing experience of our lives and others who witnessed it, too. There was no holding back, no trying to keep anything together. We told our truth, shared stories, swore, laughed, and sobbed. We mourned with abandon, and let ourselves experience joy at the same time. It helped us all.

Death is only one aspect of things to mourn. Again, loss comes in countless shapes and sizes. Health, dreams, relationships, churches, communities, jobs, animals, and faith are just a few.

While loss and grief are a natural part of the rhythms of life, unfortunately, contemporary fast-and-furious Western culture has often sent a direct message that grief is something to move through quickly, deal with, figure out, move on from. Add in toxic Christian culture, and those who feel sadness and anger are often told we are lacking in faith and need to trust God more. The result is that most people don't know what to do with grief, so we do what humans often do with uncomfortable feelings and no safe spaces to let them out—stuff them down, grit our teeth, carry on, minimize. The problem with this method is that it festers and causes even more layers of pain.

This book on practice is centered on embodying a better way, a healthier way. Part of that is the practice of mourning, learning how to honor our own losses and hold others' as well. Without healthy avenues to process loss, people fragment their experiences, neglect their real stories, numb out, and try to cope on their own, which often results in anger, depression, and anxiety. Families, churches, and organizations desperately need people who know how to practice mourning so we can become more integrated and less divided not only as individuals but also as groups.

Friday, Saturday, and Sunday Living

Years ago, The Refuge hosted an intense series during Lent that I always draw back on. Part of the experience was putting ourselves into the last three days of the Christian Holy Week on the road to Easter. We started with

Friday—the night Jesus was crucified—with a look at death. Then we moved to Saturday, the day after his death, when the sorrow, shock, and lament as the reality of loss kicks in. On Easter Sunday, we looked at the new life and hope that comes through the resurrection.

We spent the majority of the time focusing in on Friday and Saturday because they are the most overlooked days when it comes to typical Easter revelry. Yet, when we are honest, Friday and Saturday are the places we live the most. We walk in a world of brokenness, where death, shame, loss, doubt, insecurity, and confusion are parts of our typical human experience. Over the years I am continuing to learn the art of acknowledging the beauty of what I like to call *Friday, Saturday, and Sunday living*. Without death, pain, tears, and suffering, we can't really experience life. Death, sadness, life. Loss, lament, resurrection. They all bleed together in a mysterious way.

Avoiding grief only makes things worse. Pretending we don't hurt when we do only increases the likelihood of more pain later. We've got to create spaces and places for people to lament, mourn, and feel what needs to be felt to heal. We need people who can sit with us in the dark, hold our pain, and not expect us to get over it in a standardized way. I have a friend who was twenty-two when her mom died. She had a friend who actually said to her, "You get six months. Then you will be back to normal." This isn't just unhelpful. It's damaging.

We need friends who can hold us tenderly, not give advice or expect us to get better quickly. The apostle Paul, in Romans 12:15, writes, "Rejoice with those who rejoice; mourn with those who mourn" (NIV). It makes me think of the wise words of Catholic priest Henri Nouwen:

> When we honestly ask ourselves which persons in our lives mean the most to us, we often find that it is those who, instead of giving advice, solutions,

or cures, have chosen rather to share our pain and touch our wounds with a warm and tender hand. The friend who can be silent with us in a moment of despair or confusion, who can tolerate not knowing, not curing, not healing and face with us the reality of our powerlessness, that is a friend who cares.[2]

When my dad was dying, one of the greatest gifts I received were friends who didn't do anything, really, except show up, be present, and sit with us in our reality. They knew how to both rejoice and mourn. They knew that life was a wild and beautiful mix of Friday, Saturday, and Sunday.

Breaking through Denial

Many of us have heard different forms of the psychotherapist Elisabeth Kübler-Ross's Five Stages of Grief. Well-known in most circles, these five stages give a framework to the experience of grief: denial, anger, depression, bargaining, and acceptance.[3] As we journey through this chapter, keep remembering that grief is not limited to loss of a person. It is any loss, and as we engage with the practice of mourning, consider the breadth and depth of your own losses as well as those around you.

Entire books are written on the various stages of grief, but I want to primarily focus on the first stage—denial—because it opens the door to healing and deserves extra attention. There are many forms of denial—minimizing, justifying, rationalizing, rejecting, ignoring, and pretending. Do any of these coping mechanisms sound familiar to you? In different ways, I am good at all of them. Denial is what comes far more naturally to me than freely expressing grief. Initially, denial helps us cope with whatever loss we are experiencing. It can be a healthy protection mechanism at first; however, over time, denial outlasts its usefulness and begins to give us trouble personally, relationally, and spiritually.

A scene in the movie *Monty Python and the Holy Grail* illuminates denial so well. It includes a well-armored man who is being attacked by an enemy with a sword, one body part at a time. He pretends he's not injured at all, and with each new slicing off of a body part, his response trivializes the wound: "'Tis but a scratch." "It's just a flesh wound!" Pretty soon, he no longer has legs or arms, and blood is spurting everywhere. But he's fine; it's just a flesh wound. That is so me! Often, I can pretend I'm doing better than I am. It's not always false. I can remain so busy and focused on surviving that I ignore what's going on in my soul, actually believing I'm doing much better than I really am. Then, when I pause and more purposefully take notice, I realize I'm bleeding everywhere and it needs attention. Do you know this feeling? It's almost like life is too busy to feel.

Most of us are used to minimizing, justifying, rationalizing, rejecting, ignoring, or *pretending we're not in as much pain as we actually are*. It usually always harms us in the end.

A core experience of minimizing is what author and speaker Brené Brown calls "comparative suffering,"[4] where we look at what others are experiencing and find a way to squeeze down our pain in comparison. It's never good for us — or others, either. I have heard a lot of people share their pain and brush it off with, "But I know it's a first-world problem. There are people literally starving to death in Africa right now so it could be way worse." My friend Adrienne, whose four-year old son, Noah, died from a completely unknown illness, says something that reverberates in my soul: "grief can't be graded."

Learning not to minimize our own pain or the pain of others is core to the practice of mourning. The ability to do this starts with allowing ourselves to have open, broken hearts that deeply feel.

Open, Broken Hearts

One thing I've noticed over the years is that the more we become people of practice, engaged in real life with ourselves and others, the more we have to actually mourn. Years ago, I didn't feel the weight of the world because I was myopically focused on personal survival as a wife and mother maintaining a good Christian image. My world was fairly small, in retrospect. As it enlarged and I became more aware of wider systemic injustice and others' real human struggles, it has become a bit overwhelming. Now, everywhere I look I see poverty and pain, unjust systems that keep perpetuating harm to people I love. People losing people and animals they cherish, the faith they once held dear, their identities. Struggles and losses from every angle mixed into trauma from all of the political chaos in our own country, the world. Add in mass shootings in sacred places of worship, concerts, schools, and places where people are gathered to learn and play—not die—and we're constantly reminded that life is fragile and hard.

I recently watched an interesting YouTube video centered on trauma for doctors and those in helping professions. There's a special level of trauma that first-responders experience, but this piece focused on an often ignored area—secondary trauma that is related to our broken systems and the helplessness that goes along with it. This second violation often feels like too much to hold, the powerlessness too great.

Do you feel the heaviness, too?

Being people who can hold the pain of the world, our own and others, is not an easy task. The practice of mourning together, corporately, helps. In 2017, I started a group for people who are trying to navigate the realities of the Trump presidency. Many of us are exhausted, broken-hearted, and sometimes hopeless as we watch blatant discrimination rise and protective policies we value for people and our planet be systematically dismantled. Having a collective place to share has been healing for a lot of us, and almost everyone in the group says the same thing as my friend Marty: "Having this space to grieve, mourn, vent, rage, cry, and let myself express all my feelings freely has helped me survive the past several years."

Every year at The Refuge we host Blue Christmas, an evening of reflective stations created for those who struggle with the holiday season. Everyone's favorite is the anger station where we smash ornaments in a holy, reflective way. These kinds of community spaces for mourning and expressing grief help us feel less crazy, less alone in a crumbling world.

Educator and author Parker Palmer also speaks of what he calls "standing in the tragic gap" and holding space for our own broken hearts and the broken hearts of others. He says,

> There are at least two ways to understand what it means to have our hearts broken. One is to imagine the heart broken into shards and scattered about—a feeling most of us know, and a fate we would like to avoid. The other is to imagine the heart broken open into new capacity—a process that is not without pain but one that many of us would welcome. As I stand in the tragic gap between reality and possibility, this small, tight fist of a thing called my heart can break open into greater capacity to hold more of my own and the world's suffering and joy, despair and hope.[5]

I want this for my heart, for our hearts. I want our small, tight fists to break open into greater capacity to hold suffering and joy, despair and hope.

Palmer also expands on this with an old Hasidic tale that goes like this:

> The pupil comes to the rebbe and askes, "Why does the Torah tell us to 'place these words upon

your hearts'? Why does it not tell us to place the holy words in our hearts? The rebbe answers, "it is because as we are, our hearts are closed, and we cannot place the holy words in our hearts. So we place them on top of our hearts. And there they stay until, one day, the heart breaks, and the words fall in.[6]

"One day, the heart breaks, and the words fall in."

Our capacity for heartbreak is not something to run away from but to run toward. There's no need to toughen up; in fact, the world's got enough armor on already. We get how to do that. Being people with open, broken hearts is what's desperately needed.

But how do we navigate through heartbreak? Most of us aren't the best at mourning and letting the truth of our sorrow and pain out in a healthy way. We have been taught a quick turnaround after pain, often with a "trust God and focus on the positive" mindset or "go sort that out with a therapist and get back to normal" solutions. In a fast-moving world, taking time to really feel our feelings, allow ourselves room to grieve, is rare. Not all of these messages come from the outside; a lot of us also have our own internal *I shouldn't feel this way* or *I should be over this by now* messages that grief is not okay. We often think we should be stronger, better, happier, more grateful and not focus on the negative, no matter the loss.

Learning to Lament

When you think of the word *lament*, what comes to mind? For me, it's weeping, wailing, on my knees or laying on the floor, tearing sackcloth, keening. It's much more than just shedding a few tears, blowing our nose and moving on. Lament is about letting our hearts feel what needs to be felt and not trying to do a bypass on big feelings. Lament is definitely a lost art; in many cultures today (and certainly in the Old Testament that Jews and Christians share), lament is a central part of life's rhythms. It wasn't frowned upon as being unspiritual or a lack of faith or being dramatic. Men and women alike were given permission to grieve, feel, cry out, weep, wail, and retreat.

One of the reasons I love the book of Psalms is that it is filled with cries of lament, honest stories of struggle with life and God and faith and a willingness to cry out and not hold back. The Psalms illustrate that it is okay to "let it rip with God" and demonstrate a rawness that is often missing in many of our conversations. God can hack it. The question is, can we?

Lamenting helps us not move too quickly toward action, which can be our human way of trying to shortcut the rough and visceral work of lament. In conversations about justice and healing in our world, we often want to get to *what can we do?* as quickly as possible. I will always remember the wise words of Native American author and activist Mark Charles, who prophetically chastised our instinctive desire to move toward action and skip over the need for a long lament over what our nation did and still does to the Natives. We have to let ourselves feel. We have to let the heaviness set in, our hearts be stirred, broken, wrecked, grieved. Moving to action too quickly is our way of avoiding the pain, and this is one of the reasons we have so many examples of false and superficial healing.

Letting ourselves and others *go there* is vulnerable and risky, but it is what will open us up to true healing and change; it is also what will connect us to others. Contemplative author Phileena Heuertz says, "When we learn to walk in the dark, we wake up to the reality that we are knitted into an unbreakable knot of connection with God and the human family."[7] I have never felt more connected to God and the human family than we do now as we walk in the dark through the deep grief of losing our son.

Advice from a Grief Therapist

Our Refuge Kids Pastor, Stacy Schaffer, is also a grief therapist for kids. It always helps having one on staff, but I'm even more grateful for it now. Daily, she holds space for kids who are grieving the loss of a special person, the fallout of a parent's divorce, or a host of other hard things. Imagine if when we were kids we had a safe place like this to process what was swirling around inside of us; how different a lot of our lives would be. She recently shared some helpful advice with me related to holding space for our own grief and others as well:

> *Don't compare.* Everyone's pain is unique, and one of the worst things we can do is evaluate our grief by comparing our losses to others.
>
> *The Stages of Grief aren't linear.* Rather, they are a framework we keep moving through. Don't be mad at ourselves or others when we move from acceptance back to anger in a split second. It doesn't mean we didn't do our work; it just means we're feeling what needs to be felt.
>
> *Accept grief bursts.* We can learn from kids who can feel deep sadness one minute and then next thing you know it's "Squirrel!" and they're moving on to playing in the sand the next. That's not always denial; it's just going with the flow, and that's what kids do best.
>
> *Just be honest.* It's far better to admit that we don't really know what to do or say and let people know we want to be there for them. There's a greeting card by Emily McDowell (she makes the best cards ever) that sums this up so well. It says, "I'm sorry I haven't been around. I didn't know what to say."
>
> *Express through creating or body movement.* If it helps to draw, write, act, dance, or express grief in some other creative way, do it. Everything doesn't always

come through words. Our bodies store even more than our minds do.

Let go of how you're "supposed to grieve." There are no rules. Be you. Do what you need to do, how you need to do it, when you need to do it.

Core to almost everything Stacy shares with her clients is remembering the wise words of Hope Edelman, the author of *Motherless Daughters: The Legacy of Loss*: "Someone did us all a grave injustice by implying that mourning has a distinct beginning, middle, and end. That's the stuff made of short fiction. That's not real life."[8]

"Thank You for Sharing," and Don't Pass the Tissues

In our Twelve Step groups, we have a few rules that are sometimes initially awkward for people. First, there's no cross talk. This means that after people share painful truths, we just say "thank you for sharing" and move on to the next person. We don't start asking twenty questions or bust in with "Oh my God, that is so hard!" or "My heart hurts for you" or "I get what you're saying because (insert my story)" or any of the things that might be rattling around in our heads. Rather, we sit with their brave words and simply say, "Thank you for sharing." It can be unnerving, but it's an exceptionally helpful practice because it holds us back from making our anxiety about people's pain more important than people's actual pain. I love this rule because it forces us to trust God, trust others, to resist our tendency to make pain about us, and instead let people share freely.

When someone's crying, we also don't hand them a tissue. Wait, what? What if snot is dripping from their nose? I get our desire to be a good friend, but passing tissues in that moment sends a subtle but powerful message: *Please stop crying. Here you go, blow, pull it together.* We don't mean to. It's not intentional and the desire to help a sniffly friend is honorable. However, part of becoming healthier holders of sacred space for people means letting others fully feel, not shutting them down, and not making their pain about us. At The Refuge we try to always have tissues (or at least toilet paper because we're classy like that) somewhere in the room so people can grab them when they want, but our practice is clear — *listen well and never hand out an unsolicited tissue.*

While holding emotional space for people is an important part of the practice of mourning, sometimes we need to be physically held, too. In a culture of independence, figuring things out on our own, and oversexualizing each other, this part often gets missed. But sometimes we just need to be held.

Years ago, when our surviving college-aged twin, Jonas, was about eighteen months old and wanted either Jose or I to hold him, he would toddle up to us with his sweet chubby legs, raise both hands, and say "Hold you." He kept his hands reached toward us until we picked him up.

"Hold you."

Because sometimes we just need to be held.

In the flesh.

By a living, breathing person.

Here.

Now.

What I loved about Jonas's *hold you* is that he knew exactly what he needed and asked for it. He didn't sit and wait for us to notice. He didn't hesitate or think he was stupid for asking. He didn't assume we'd pick up on the cues. Instead, he did what kids do (and why they are leaders in all-things-spiritual), and asked for what he wanted — to be held.

Because sometimes we just need to be held.

Mike's wife died when his kids were teenagers. Now in his seventies, he has lived alone a long time, finding a way to be a widower by cultivating meaningful friendships across genders. He's also become a hugger because for a lot of people hugs are healing. Hugs are a way he's navigated his grief for many decades. One of our friends coined the term, "The kingdom of God is like a Mike hug." While I have spent the majority of my life married with a whole bunch of kids constantly needing to be held and helped, Mike has illuminated how many people go long distances of time with no human touch at all. None. This void only magnifies losses. I read that there are now cuddle services in some cities where people pay good money just to be held. It's easy to jump to *but that's so weird* in our minds if we are in a relationship where we have physical touch, but it's not a strange need for those who are alone, hurting, and mourning the loss of people or dreams of the way they thought life would be.

There are a whole lot of people in this world in desperate need of being held. Maybe you are? I'm not suggesting going around imposing hugs on people who look like they need one; but I am challenging us to consider how we can offer healthy and secure physical connection with other humans in need of it. It can be a powerful addition to the practice of mourning. Adults don't go wandering around saying, "Hold you" with their actual words even if they desperately want to.

Less and More

Remember, none of the practices in this book are formulaic or scientific. They are only a framework to consider, skills to integrate, and creative ways to move differently in relationship with ourselves, others, the world. They are ideas to try to embody. I sometimes like to consider possibilities through the lens of *what if we practiced less of this, more of that?* What if we became people who offered less of some unhelpful things and more of what facilitates healing and connection?

When it comes to the practice of mourning, there are some tangible things we can do less and more of. Read this list below and consider which might be easier or harder for you.

— *Less talking, more presence.* Often we have an unconscious hope that if we could say the right words in the exact right way, it would radically help another person. Most people aren't one sentence away from feeling better when they are grieving. Presence seems to matter the most.

— *Less advice, more questions.* It's a natural default to talk instead of listen. Questions usually save us from advice giving and fixing. They help people process out loud and take a lot of pressure off us coming up with the right words that can't be found anyway.

— *Less anxiety, more trust.* When people are hurting, we have an instinct to fix it or do-something-do-anything that will help the hurting person feel better in that moment. Letting go of that is always a good idea. Really, that is just another way to make it about us.

— *Less perfection, more grace.* We will screw up with people, say lame things, or fail our friends. I recently gave unsolicited advice to a hurting friend. As soon as the words tumbled out of my mouth, I knew they would hurt instead of help so I took care of it in that moment and said, "Sorry, I know that's not what you need right now." We need grace as friends, leaders, people.

What are some things you're learning to do less of, more of, as you hold your own pain and the pain of others?

Kintsugi, Golden Repair

Years ago a friend told me about the traditional Japanese art form of kintsugi, where a precious metal is used to bring together the pieces of a broken pottery item and transform it into something whole and beautiful. The breaks aren't covered up; rather they are honored and illuminated. "Kin" means golden and "tsugi" means repair. Together it means "golden repair." *Golden repair.*

Maybe this is the essence of the practice of mourning—bringing together the broken pieces and enhancing the breaks.

I have many kintsugi pieces of life over the years. Shame, pain, failures, flops, shattered dreams, and the hard ugly things real life brings that over time have been pieced together through golden repair. They have become integrated into my story, not neat and tidy or wrapped with a tiny bow. Rather, broken, shattered, beautiful and whole at the same time. My guess is you do, too.

Making beauty from the brokenness is part of our work in the world. Like everything, it starts with us. We can't pass on what we aren't willing to experience ourselves. As we embrace our losses instead of try to rush through grief, and learn to hold others in their pain as well, not only will we be transformed but we will help others heal as well. We will become people of golden repair, bringing together the broken pieces and enhancing the breaks.

In her book *Sacred Wounds*, my friend Teresa Pasquale speaks of the Buddhist philosophy based on lotus and mud. She writes,

> The lotus flower is a beautiful and bright symbol of life, but the lotus grows out of the mud in swamps. There is no lotus without the mud—there is no joy without suffering; there is no transformation without grief. Buddhist images and metaphors of the mud and the lotus remind us that in the dankest, darkest, most messy places is born one of the most beautiful flowers on earth.[9]

Friday-Saturday-Sunday living, learning to lament, open and broken hearts, holding each other, golden repair, lotus and mud. The practice of mourning is messy and beautiful.

It's often avoided and deeply missing in our world. Francis Weller, a grief therapist and speaker, says "The work of the mature person is to carry grief in one hand and gratitude in the other and to be stretched large by them."[10]

Let's be people who honor our own pain and the pain of others, who can hold grief in one hand, gratitude in the other. Let's keep being stretched large, together.

Our focus on grief and loss isn't contained only in the practice of mourning; it will also help us as we move on to our next practice together—failing. No one likes to flail, flounder, fail, but it's part of being human and we sure could use some help in learning how to practice it more freely.

A PRAYER FOR MOURNING

God, help us learn to lament and grieve.
May we be a safe container for others who are mourning.
May we hold our friends in the dark, and let them hold us, too.
May we bring together our broken pieces, making the breaks beautiful.
Amen.

FOR PERSONAL REFLECTION

1. Think of the movements of Friday-Saturday-Sunday living—death-grief-new life, loss-lament-resurrection. Where have you seen this pattern in your own story?

2. What are some losses you are grieving? How do you relate to minimizing them or being mad at yourself for not being better yet? How can you be more gentle with yourself?

3. If you're grieving some losses—no matter how big or small—take some time and process by writing a short psalm or piece for lament. Here are some prompts:

> *God, right now, I feel . . .*
> *My heart is heavy with . . .*
> *My eyes can't see . . .*
> *My ears can't hear . . .*
> *My fingers can't touch . . .*
> *I'm so sad about . . .*
> *I'm weary of . . .*
> *I hope that once again I can feel . . .*

4. Consider what might be a piece of kintzugi—golden repair—in your life, something broken that is being transformed.

FOR GROUP REFLECTION

1. Share with the group what stirred up in you as you engaged with the practice of mourning. What feelings did you notice?

2. Forms of denial include *minimizing, justifying, rationalizing, rejecting, ignoring, pretending*. Think of pain and losses in your life; which of these forms of denial are familiar to you? How are you learning to break out of denial and feel more deeply?

3. What are some things you are learning to lament in this season (your own pain, others', social justice issues)? What is that experience like for you?

4. Read the list of "Less and More" in the practice of mourning. What are you trying to practice in your own story and experience? What other possibilities would you add?
5. As a group, do the lament exercise in the Personal Reflection section and share out loud. Consider a story in your life that's a kintsugi piece, something that was broken and made beautiful. Share with the group.

TO PRACTICE

1. Share your real story of grief and loss with someone. Don't minimize it, rationalize it, or portray it as something you've got figured out. Practice what it feels like to be really honest and sit with *it just hurts*.
2. Next time you listen to someone's pain, try not to add in comments like "It's going to be okay" or hand them tissues. Just thank them for sharing, being present with them, and holding space freely. Notice what it feels like.
3. Apply one of the "Less and More" principles into a relationship and reflect how it impacted your experience.
4. Next time there is a public vigil for a local, national, or global tragedy, attend it and participate in mourning with others. Notice what you learn from your experience.

DIG DEEPER

Bearing the Unbearable: Love, Loss, and the Heartbreaking Path of Grief by Joanne Cacciatore

The Cure for Sorrow: A Book of Blessings in Times of Grief by Jan Richardson

The Inner Voice of Love: A Journey through Anguish to Freedom by Henri J. M. Nouwen

It's OK That You're Not OK: Meeting Grief and Loss in a Culture That Doesn't Understand by Megan Devine

The Wild Edge of Sorrow: Rituals of Renewal and the Sacred Work of Grief by Francis Weller

CHAPTER 8

THE PRACTICE OF FAILING

Fail—fāl
Verb / present participle: *failing*
1. To be unsuccessful in meeting the desired outcome
2. To miss the mark
3. To be unable to do something after repeated attempts

Gmorning!
You're gonna make mistakes.

—Lin-Manuel Miranda

The year was 2007 and I was walking the floor of the international Christian book conference preparing for a signing for my second book, which was a spiritual formation tool for evangelical Christian women that offered what a lot of them didn't have—places for honest and vulnerable stories and truth telling. The material is much different than what I'd write today, but I was proud of its unique contribution and that the publisher had hopes for a four-book series. I was checking out the long winding aisles of booths stacked with shiny new merchandise and books when I got a call from my publisher. She had received a disturbing call from their primary Christian book retailer. When they discovered I was a co-lead pastor, they decided to withdraw their large and lucrative order, refusing to sell it because of theological convictions about female leadership. It was a kick in the gut. For a few minutes I couldn't breathe. Then I caught a gulp of air and immediately started cussing like a sailor (nice, on the floor of a Christian conference), awash with shame and anger, feeling like a failure. Simply for being female.

It's not that I hadn't experienced failures in different ways before, but this particular one had a hard and painful edge. It magnified the risk I had taken to become a female pastor with evangelical roots and the vulnerability of my own story and the stories of others I told in the book. The mix was a bad cocktail that rocked my soul. It made me want to run for the hills and never write another word again. Failing can have that effect on us. Henri Nouwen, in his book *Can You Drink the Cup?*, says, "When we are crushed like grapes, we cannot think of the wine we will become."[2] In that moment, with happy, energized people buzzing around on the conference floor, buying books and cutting new deals, I wasn't thinking of the wine I would become.

I felt completely crushed.

Failing is part of the human experience, yet, there aren't many places to talk about failure and embrace it as a natural part of life. Failed relationships, faith, dreams, parenting, jobs, and finances are a few in the long list of ways things often come apart in real life, don't work out the way we hoped, and cause us to hang our heads, hide, and beat ourselves up mentally over and over again. *Why couldn't we be better? What if we had only* (fill in the blank)? *What's wrong with us?*

This chapter is about the practice of failing, of learning to embrace failure as a part of being human, cultivating resilience, and learning to stand back up over and over again. It's about remembering that failing means we are in the game—playing, living, loving, risking, trying. We are sure to *fail* at all of the practices we've talked about so far, and owning our stories instead of hiding or running from them is part of the shared human experience.

We've All Got a Failure Story

Brené Brown, whose voice continues to encourage so many to risk failure in our lives, says,

> If we're going to put ourselves out there and love with our whole hearts, we're going to experience heartbreak. If we're going to try new, innovative things, we're going to fail. If we're going to risk caring and engaging, we're going to experience disappointment. . . . When we own our stories, we avoid being trapped as characters in stories someone else is telling.[3]

Our stories of failure need to be told, but because failing is often deeply connected to shame, it makes them difficult to talk about.

My friend Steve was a single dad who lost his job in a high-profile Christian ministry and was left with deep shame over not being able to provide for his family the way he had been trained to believe was right. Patriarchy doesn't just hurt women. The pressure that men feel to succeed in a way that is socially acceptable can be crushing. As he untangled the damaging messages of the dominant male culture (with an extra measure of Christian male pressure), he entered into therapy and uncovered a web of fear and insecurity he didn't even know existed. He began to talk more freely about what he had been carrying and how deeply embedded the message of being a failure had damaged his soul. He's been doing inner work that started with more bravely sharing his story and breaking through the ravages of shame. It's not easy, but he's finding healing.

Some of our closest lifelong friends adopted a daughter out of foster care when she was four years old. For her entire childhood, they poured their lives into offering her a life of security and resource, ensuring she had the proper medical and emotional care to help heal some of her deep psychological wounds and provide every possible opportunity for success. After years of sacrifice, suffering, and sleepless nights as parents, she left home and never came back. It's now been several years since she disappeared from their lives. Daily, they wonder if she's alive, if they'll ever hear from her again. After eighteen years of effort, they are seemingly left with nothing but heartache. In our countless conversations about our shared struggles as parents, we always land in the same place—there's nothing they could have done differently but it sucks that this is what they're left with.

Even after all these years of intimate friendship with us, it's not easy for them to tell their story. They are often tired of thinking about it and dwelling on it, tired of the space it's taken in their lives, and tired of replaying all the things they wish could have turned out differently.

I know the "I just don't want to talk about it anymore" feeling well.

For me, I have been healing from the fallout of a failed relationship, a friendship I invested over a decade of blood, sweat, and guts in and that is now irrevocably broken. If I counted the hours I spent agonizing over my anger, sadness, and shame related to it, it would probably add up to years. Then I get mad at myself for spending so much unnecessary time on it, flogging myself for being a failure at healing, too. Do you know this feeling? The energy spent reiterating failures, beating ourselves up because things didn't turn out the way we expected?

These same kinds of failure stories are being played out in all of our lives, usually with a similar thread but distinctive twists. Marriages that didn't work after count-less years of effort and thousands of dollars of therapy, failed business endeavors that left us bankrupt, exposed, or feeling like losers, delinquent children in trouble with the law or struggling in life after we loved them with our whole hearts, bombing out of college, getting fired from a job, or foreclosing on a house and hoping no one will find out. Maybe it's hidden addictions to food, drugs, alcohol, or porn that we keep trying to get free from but just can't seem to or all the mixed-up feelings about failing as a parent over and over again. Like all things related to shame, we usually do whatever we can to manage our response to failure on our own. We push it down, carry on, and try to figure it out alone so that others don't know how devas-tated we actually feel inside.

Yet, the first, most critical step for each of the practices in this book seems to be the same: Own our stories first. Acknowledge them, embrace them, and use them for good.

Failure is part of being human.

We're Only Human after All

Even though it's easy to say, embracing our humanness is complicated for a lot of us. Many have been taught that with the right kind of effort we can rise above our ordinary humanness and conquer our fears through strength and confidence. A lot of us are also perfectionists, needing to get it right to feel okay about ourselves.

It makes me think of the sage words of one of my all-time favorite writers who always beautifully captures the honest human experience, Anne Lamott. She says,

> Perfectionism is the voice of the oppressor, the enemy of the people. It will keep you cramped and insane your whole life, and it is the main obstacle between you and a shitty first draft. I think perfectionism is based on the obsessive belief that if you run carefully

enough, hitting each stepping-stone just right, you won't have to die. The truth is that you will die anyway and that a lot of people who aren't even looking at their feet are going to do a whole lot better than you, and have a lot more fun while they're doing it.[4]

Perfectionism is not only exhausting, it's also paralyzing. How many of you haven't done certain things that you really wanted to try out of fear of not getting it right?

Often, most of us aren't taught to honor our humanity, frailty, limitations, or how to embrace failure. This doesn't mean settling or limiting what's possible as people. Humanity is awesome, doing incredible things in the world for generations. But we're still flesh-and-blood humans who make mistakes, screw things up, end up in places we never thought we'd be.

Some of us have an added message that if we prayed and worked hard enough for God we wouldn't fail, that our performance was somehow attached to our faith (or lack of it). Oh, the Bible verses I have in my head that back up that false thinking. I remember years ago when I was a counseling student at seminary and had a very difficult client with a major personality disorder. I shared with the women's group at my church how hard it was, the emotional toll it was taking on me every week to enter into the room as a professional. One of the women's very first responses was: "Well, have you prayed about it?" Really, that's what you've got? My blood rose to boiling, and I shot back, "Are you freaking kidding me? Do you honestly think I haven't tried that a thousand times already? It's *just hard* for goodness sake!" This is also why cross talk in groups is so unhealthy; it usually always leaves people feeling like failures somehow: "Have you tried this? Have you done that?"

We often associate anything that's hard with *something we did wrong*. There are a lot of things in the world that are just plain hard and have nothing to do with what we did or didn't do, prayed or didn't pray. Embracing that reality in the practice of failing is a good idea.

One time I was speaking at a popular Christian conference and was asked a question that I misinterpreted and completely flubbed the answer. It was related to race and privilege and was horribly humiliating because in that moment I couldn't fix it, steal the microphone back, and make it right. I had to live with the shame and pain of making a huge mistake in front of everyone, with all its churn and *Oh my God, how could I have said that?* tumbling around in my head like laundry in the dryer, cycling over and over again. Some of you know this feeling too.

It's the worst.

That night, alone in my room with that sick feeling rooted deeply in my stomach, I called my husband and some dear friends who understand failing and told them what happened. I wanted to escape, run, change my plane ticket and fly home to safety as quickly as I could. But, alas, that wasn't an option. Instead, I surprised myself and actually applied (in the moment) one of the most important skills I learned in recovery over the years —*embrace my humanness*. Shit happens. Life is not linear, and we screw things up unintentionally. Part of embodying something different is to live with our failures, breathe through them, honor whatever happened as a really hard thing, and carry on. I tossed and turned all night, anxious and fitful, but the next morning I did what I truly didn't want to do — got dressed, held my head high, walked back into the conference, and carried on. It's not that I didn't have big feelings, wasn't on the verge of tears all day, didn't remain keenly aware of how much shame was swirling around in my head and heart. My mantra was what I needed to remember — *I'm just human. I'm just human. I'm just human.*

And humans make mistakes.

A core piece of the practice of failing is embracing our humanity. Owning it, leaning into it, wearing it, and remembering we are in good company with a whole bunch of other humans who are also struggling with feelings of failure. My insightful friend Joanna, a spiritual director who lived in the slums of India for several years, shared these sage words with me recently, "Self-compassion is embracing our humanity, owning that we are a muddled mix of dust and divinity."

Dust and divinity.

That's me, that's you, that's all of us.

The *What ifs* and *I Sucks*

My friend Phyllis Mathis is a therapist, life coach, and healer in my life. Every Monday morning—rain, snow, sleet, or sunshine—we walk three and a half miles together; it's free therapy for both of us, and we've integrated it into our schedule for many years. She also facilitates a workshop at The Refuge one Saturday morning a month called School of Life. Centered on personal transformation, she talks about things most of us are thinking and feeling in a safe and brave space. Years ago, she shared a short piece on how all roads in our heads and hearts lead to two primary messages that cause us a lot of trouble—first, shame and the message of "I suck" and, second, fear and the circle of "What ifs?" The big idea is that shame and fear pervade the human experience. There's a relief that comes from having language for it, that we're not the only ones struggling.

I suck and *What if* swirl around in a lot of our heads. All. The. Time. Think about what's going on in your own head. Does it have a circle of critics, lined up reminding you of all your shortcomings, failures, messes, mistakes, stumbles and bumbles, and how stupid you are—or a gentle voice of care and compassion? Most everyone I know, myself included, are more familiar with the critics who usually tell me I suck. The *What ifs* center on a lot of things related to failure—What if I can't do it? What if I fail? What if they leave me? What if they don't like me? What if I actually don't have the stuff to pull it off? What if, what if, what if.

The *I suck* and *What if* cul-de-sacs are ones that human beings circle around, wasting a lot of time and energy. Saying "But that's not true—you don't suck and you'll survive any of the *What ifs*" won't make us magically have peace. But greater honesty seems to help.

The way out of the *I sucks* and *What ifs* is to say out loud: "Yep, that's what's going on in my thoughts. This is what I'm afraid of. This is what I'm thinking, feeling, and experiencing." One of our best antidotes for shame and fear loops related to failure is turning on the flood lights, exposing some of our true and vulnerable feelings, and not traveling alone in our minds anymore.

This is also why Twelve Step groups are so effective at changing lives. We learn to stop hiding all our thoughts from others. Mike, who we met in the previous chapter on mourning, also has over a decade of sobriety from sexual addiction. Trapped for over forty years in its shameful grip, he did what so many people are afraid of doing—said it out loud to a group of other people and acknowledged how much he struggled. He started with a group of safe men in his recovery group and then one day was brave enough to tell me personally. He was shaking in his shoes, as I was the first woman he'd shared it with. I can still see his watery blue eyes and shaking hands, and hear his fluttery voice as the words tumbled out. When he was done, I hugged him tightly and shared these simple words: "Thank you for sharing. I am with you." He describes what happened afterward this way, "Something shifted in me when I said it out loud and was met with love and not rejection. I experienced a freedom from the cloud of feeling like a miserable failure and began to believe that maybe I was someone worth loving." When the lights got turned on and he spoke his truth out loud, the *I suck* message he had lived with for years lost some of its power. Shame grows in the dark.

Part of the practice of failure involves acknowledging what's rattling around in our heads and hearts—the *I sucks* and the *What ifs*—instead of trying to manage them on our own.

Cultivating Resilience

I love the word *resilience*. My working definition of *resilience* is the ability to navigate adversity, failure, and change with as much health as possible. It's the ability to absorb pain and struggle but not let it kill us. It's a bounce-back-ness that isn't fake or denying of reality but deep and tangible. It's somehow, in the often-recited words from Alcoholic Anonymous, "meeting calamity with serenity."

Years ago, some of our best friends were adopting two elementary-age boys from Ethiopia and were pouring over resources to prepare. One of the books challenged them to think of ways they could develop *connection, resilience, and identity* in their kids for the transition. These words have stuck with me ever since. The need for connection, resilience, and identity is not unique to African orphans; it's something that needs to be cultivated in all of us as we become healthier human beings. These three things also help us navigate failure. When we have connected relationships and are rooted in a strong identity as a human made in the image of God, loved and worthy, it helps with resilience.

I've known my friend Tami for going on two decades now. A trauma survivor, she struggles with mental illness and sometimes has to be hospitalized to get the care she needs. Years ago, she would remain in dark places not just for months but for years. It was painful to watch but I saw her courage, tenacity, and unwillingness to give in to her illness. She says, "These hard things in life have shown me that I'm stronger than I ever thought before. I am stronger than I seemed, and have become stronger through every storm. It's surprised me and others, too." She is one of the greatest examples of resilience I can think of. Yes, she still has some bad runs and ends up needing some extra care, but the time for bounce back is now measured in days and weeks instead of years.

That's resilience.

Another way to frame resilience is a term that author Susan David uses: "emotional agility."[5] It's an ability to navigate emotions in a healthier, more fluid way. I've watched Tami and many others in my life become more emotionally agile, and it's a much-needed skill in the practice of failing.

When we fall, when we fail, we've got to keep learning to stand back up not just with our legs, but in our spirit, our souls.

As a female pastor, I have encountered countless weird moments where I got knocked to my knees—canceling me as a speaker at a community baccalaureate because of pushback from conservative pastors, memorial services I couldn't officiate in particular churches, and being called the pastor's assistant are just a few. Each and every time, I wanted to crawl for the door and find an escape route out of the church, out of feeling so exposed, out of the shame (is this pattern starting to sound familiar?). But each time, I stood back up. I know many of you have been knocked down but keep standing back up, too. It makes me think of this Chinese proverb: "If you get up one more time than you fall, you will make it through."

We have to stand up every time we get knocked down. We have to stand up when we feel like maybe we were meant to crawl. We have to stand up when shame flushes our face.

We have to stand up when we hear a voice in our head that tells us we are supposed to sit. We have to stand up even when our legs become very tired.

The battles we're each fighting look different for all of us, and the issues we care about aren't the same. For me, I have to keep fighting for dignity, equality, and restoration in this world no matter what. I keep learning that there's no way to do this without adversity, pain, and sometimes feeling chopped at the knees and wondering if it's all really worth it. What are the things you deeply care about, that you stand for, knowing you will still get knocked down?

Part of the practice of failing is learning to stand back up, over and over again. We won't want to. We get tired. We want to quit. We can't bear the thought of risking ourselves again.

But here's the greatest part—we don't have to try to stand up alone. The practice of failing requires help from others. Like Aaron holding his brother Moses' hands up when he became weary in the Old Testament book of Exodus, our friends can lift us back up again and again and stand alongside us, shoulder to shoulder, toe to toe, hearts supporting hearts, hands lifting heads.

Joanna lived in the Kolkata slums for several years. It turned out to be a traumatic experience on many levels, and she had to return to the United States to take care of her mental and physical health. It was devastating. Part of the pain for her was that complete success or complete failure were the only two truths she knew. In her world, coming off the mission field on the verge of a breakdown meant failure, that something was wrong with *her*. As she entered the path of healing, good friends helped expand her thinking. She shares, "They filled in the colors and nuances in my mind that only saw in black and white. They called out the truth in me that I forgot or was painfully distorted." They helped Joanna crawl when she couldn't yet walk. Eventually, through a lot of therapy and support, she's now in a much more stable place. However, it didn't take weeks or months; it took years. Sometimes that's how long it takes to stand again.

My husband and I run a small nonprofit called #water-heals, which is dedicated to water sports empowerment for the soul. It is our life force during the summer. We take people who don't normally have access to a boat on the water to learn to water ski, wake and knee-board, and surf. It's incredible to watch, the fear that is conquered when people lower themselves into the water and say, "I'll try." Stacy is in her thirties and had never done any water sports until she moved to Colorado. Her goal was to learn to water ski, which isn't the easiest thing to do as an adult. For eight straight seasons, she tried with no avail. We gave her every tip we could think of, and, still, she couldn't get out of the water. Honestly, I thought she'd give up after a couple of seasons, but she was determined. Two years ago—after hundreds of attempts over many years—it finally came together and she got up, fully riding on water skis with the hugest smile on her face you've ever seen. Just thinking about it now brings joy to my heart. Her tenacity is incredibly rare. Most people try a few times, get mad at themselves for not *getting it*, and call it a day.

Yet, this kind of vulnerability and passion that Stacy embodied is the essence of the practice of failing. She learned so much each of those years of trying that wasn't evidenced in reaching a goal. It's annoying, but it's true—life is not just about the end result, it's about the process, too.

Failing at Faith

Often we talk about failures on a personal and relational level and forget about what it feels like to fail spiritually. Not everyone can relate, but much of my work for the past chunk of years has been journeying with people who have experienced a faith unraveling, where everything we once knew about God and faith comes apart and we aren't sure which end is up. When our faith unravels we can feel like we are failing. Read below and see if any of these describe you right now:

— You exited *church as you knew it* and now feel on the outside.
— You no longer know how to pray, read the Bible, or connect with God in a way that feels meaningful.

— You are experiencing anger, sadness, and confusion after years of certainty and clarity about your faith.
— You have broken relationships with friends and family.
— You feel lonely and disconnected where once there was joy, purpose, and a sense of community.
— You feel shame that you just can't *figure it out.*

My Canadian friend and popular author and blogger, Sarah Bessey, describes it this way: "Nothing is quite where it belongs anymore. Everything moved . . . or maybe you moved. Either way, you feel disoriented."[6] For a lot of us, clarity has turned to confusion, security to feeling on shaky ground, and our ability to articulate our faith has dissolved into a foreign language we can't speak. As the wider church continues to shift and find its way, more people I intersect with relate to failing at faith.

I met my friend Janet in an online class I co-facilitate called Walking Wounded: Hope and Healing for Those Hurt by Church and Ministry. She served in third-world countries for years, working as a Bible translator alongside her husband. Through many twists and turns, her faith crumbled, their marriage dissolved, and she lost her passion for all she had given her life to. Now a divorced, former Christian wife and missionary, she is rebuilding her life as a single, professional woman who is unsure what she believes anymore and considers herself on the bubble between atheism and agnosticism. Other people she used to be in lockstep with are doing just fine in their faith, making it easy for her to wonder: *What's wrong with me?*

The thing that often gives us the most trouble related to failed faith—and really, all types of failure—is comparing ourselves to others. We look at friends and family who are still connected, thriving, doing what we used to do. We see others mastering skills we bombed at. We see people pulling off marriages and successful jobs we failed in. We see the success of other kids while ours are struggling and wonder if it's our fault. No matter what it is, comparing ourselves to others will always result in shame and pain.

I constantly remind people that there's no such thing as failed faith. It might feel real but it comes from the unhealthy binary, either/or thinking many of us were taught in rigid systems. It becomes embedded in our hearts and experience and will always give us trouble. Thinking we're either in or out, right or wrong, on God's good side or bad side, will always lead to pain and strife. Making peace with an evolving faith—that we will always be changing, growing, morphing our spirituality—is an important practice that isn't readily taught in a lot of churches.

Some of you don't struggle with your faith and maybe cannot relate to this personally, but you can still help others with this practice. In fact, you can be a powerful source of healing for people when it comes to these issues of faith. Here's how: *Learn how to honor others' diverse and uncertain faith stories with tenderness and care.* Let them wrestle and struggle and resist your temptation to try to fix their complex questions and doubts with simple solutions. Don't worry about family and friends when they stop going to church or start saying things about God you don't agree with. Try to trust God's work in their lives and affirm your heart for them through less words and more presence.

The Flogging Machine

Elizabeth Gilbert, in her book *Big Magic: Creative Living Beyond Fear*, reminds us: "Whatever you do, try not to dwell too long on your failures. You don't need to conduct autopsies on your disasters."[7] I am so good at these kinds of autopsies, and I usually do them in what I call the flogging machine.

You may have your own word for it, but I consider the *flogging machine* the place we go in our heads to beat ourselves up after we make some kind of mistake (no matter how small or big), experience uncomfortable conflict, or perceive we are failing.

Each of us is different, but my flogging machine seems to have these pieces of equipment in it:

— a bat, to beat myself up with
— a megaphone to blast the negative messages over and over about myself
— a group of judges; people evaluating and critiquing me
— a tape recorder that keeps replaying and rewinding the conversation, the thing I said or did wrong, over and over again
— special earplugs that tune out anything good

What does your flogging machine look like, the place you go when you fail? Part of embodying something different is dismantling this kind of negative, debilitating power in our lives and traveling lighter. It doesn't mean we don't take a trip into the flogging machine now and then, but it means we stop hiding out there for too long as a way of avoiding our next failure.

You may not relate, but I'm quite sure you're in relationship with someone who is familiar with the flogging machine. We can help people stay out of it by acknowledging its pull. I have a friend who sometimes knows I might be struggling with something I said or did at The Refuge, so he'll text me, "Don't go into the flogging machine tonight. It's not worth it."

Instead of beating ourselves up, let's consider how we can use our perceived failures for good. Regret of any size is a time-waster, a sucker of souls, and robber of our thoughts. Left at just regret, we can get stuck. We can't change the past. No matter how hard we will it, replay it, rethink it, regret it, we cannot and will not ever be able to change the past. Circular regret and replaying failure loops won't get us anywhere new. It won't make our kids be different. Heal a broken relationship. Bring back someone from the dead. Get us that job back. Erase a memory. Change another person. Make our faith magically reappear.

What we can do, however, is consider using what we've learned to participate in nurturing a different future. A much healthier way is to own what's happened in the past with as honest of eyes as possible and add the most important clause we can to it: _____ *happened, but I can learn* _____ *from it.*

Yep, I wish I had . . . I could have . . . I tried that and failed . . . but I can learn _____ from it.

This is central to the practice of failing. We can honor our humanity, our ongoing stories that are always unfolding and that we are always learning. We can remember good comes from evil, light from darkness, beauty from ashes. We can honor that everything we've done is an opportunity to grow, and life usually isn't how we imagined.

We can ask better questions related to our alleged failures to help us keep stumbling and bumbling our way forward. Here are some to consider:

— How can we offer ourselves compassion?
— How can we learn from the past so we can forge a different future?
— What can we personally practice differently moving forward?
— What are we more clear on now?
— What are we now unwilling to do that once came so easy?
— What are we currently open to that we once resisted?
— What has the pain taught us about ourselves? God? Life?
— What can we put into practice that is healthier, wiser, less codependent or controlling, no matter how tiny the step?
— And because good usually emerges from hard places, what good come out of it? What can you look back to

now and say "Even in the ugliest parts of this story,
emerged?"

What are some other questions that help you process
through failure in a more healthy way? Whatever they are,
keep asking them.

We started this chapter with the words of Broadway
producer, singer, and actor Lin-Manuel Miranda, the writer
and star of *Hamilton*, who I am guessing knows a thing or
two about vulnerability, risk, and failure. His rhymes about
mistakes, trials, and failures are true and challenging, but
they end with an admonition that will help us persevere:
"REST UP."[8]

That's where we're going next together—the practice of
resting. Each of these practices are taxing in multiple ways.
We definitely won't last if we don't take time for self-care,
renewal, and rest.

A PRAYER FOR FAILING

God, we admit we're often afraid to fail.
Remind us of our humanness.
Strengthen our resilience.
Give us courage to stand back up, again and again.
Help us be people who are willing to risk, try, fail.
Amen.

FOR PERSONAL REFLECTION

1. What are failures in your life that are hard to talk about? What prevents you from being more honest about them?
2. What are some ways you've been cultivating resilience in your life, bouncing back faster from hard things?
3. Do you have a *flogging machine* you enter when you fail? What does yours look like, feel like?
4. Consider a recent failure, something that you wished you had done differently. Try to apply some of the questions that are listed on pages 177–78.

FOR GROUP REFLECTION

1. If you feel safe enough, share with the group a failure that is hard for you to talk about. What makes it difficult to share freely? How do you feel, saying it out loud? Share these reflections with the group.
2. Create a space to offer any perspectives on feeling like we've failed at faith. Read the list of possible feelings and experiences and share in that section any you relate to. If you don't connect with them personally, try to listen to those who do without fixing in any way.
3. Share what your *flogging machines* are like. What can you learn from one another that will help you spend less time in them?
4. Review the questions we can ask ourselves to reframe perceived failure. Which are most helpful to you? What other ones would you add?

TO PRACTICE

1. Think of something you really want to try but you've been afraid to, no matter how small or big. How can you take a step toward it, letting yourself risk your heart, time, the possibility of failure?
2. Share a painful failure story out loud with someone — at work, church, home, with a friend. It might seem insignificant or feel uncomfortable or unnecessary to rehash but it is part of normalizing failure and bringing it into the light.
3. Practice reframing your thinking around experiences of failure or disappointment. Try this guided prompt and see where it leads:

I consider myself to have failed when

_____

That situation made/makes me feel

_____

But, through this situation, I learned/am learning

_____

I know that, no matter what, God

_____

I know that these good things are still true about me:

_____

The next time I feel as if I have failed, I will remember

_____

DIG DEEPER

Big Magic: Creative Living beyond Fear by Elizabeth Gilbert
*Carry On, Warrior: The Power of Embracing Your Messy, Beauti-
ful Life* by Glennon Doyle Melton
*The Gifts of Imperfection: Let Go of Who You Think You're Sup-
posed to Be and Embrace Who You Are* by Brené Brown
Self-Compassion: The Proven Power of Being Kind to Yourself by
Kristin Neff

CHAPTER 9

***

THE PRACTICE
OF RESTING

Rest—rest
Verb / present participle: **resting**
1. To create space to be still
2. To stop striving
3. To let go of the worries of the world

Rest and be thankful.
—William Wordsworth

I often facilitate groups and gatherings that involve a wide variety of people sharing stories and real life. Sometimes I start with asking, "How are you feeling right now?" And then give an opportunity for everyone to respond out loud with a one or two-word feeling. Almost always, some of the responses usually include *tired, weary, worn down, exhausted,* or *overwhelmed* but they are mixed with a bunch of other words. However, universally, when I'm in a room of helpers, advocates, and people who are practicing their faith in a really tangible way (oh, and single moms), these are by far the most popular feelings.

Tired, weary, worn down, exhausted, overwhelmed.

Do any of these feel familiar to you right now?

We've been journeying through some really challenging practices together, ways of moving in the world that require a lot of emotional and physical energy. We can often become so focused on tangible care, connection, or advocacy with others that we neglect our own souls. Author and spiritual director Phileena Heuertz sums up what is true for many of us in this simple sentence: "We tend to take better care of others than we do ourselves."[1]

We tend to take better care of others than we do ourselves.

Does this feel true for you? It sure does for me. I am a natural at encouraging others to practice self-care and rest but when it comes to practicing it myself, it's often a different story. We can't expect ourselves to be people of practice and not rest. It's not only unhealthy and unwise for ourselves; it's a sure way to harm others as well. When we don't rest, we end up burning out, checking out, ditching relationships, and bailing out of hard situations instead of staying in. I've seen many people go all-in on incarnational endeavors where they spend a lot of time rescuing people on the side of the road bleeding and then end up on the side of the road in need of help themselves.

I have a friend who often says, "Don't forget, even God rested." The Old Testament story describing God's creation reminds us, "And on the seventh day God finished the work that he had done, and he rested on the seventh day from all the work that he had done" (Gen. 2:2). This call to rest was included in the Ten Commandments, and a Sabbath day remains a core practice in the Jewish tradition. Many times in the Gospels, Jesus separates himself from the group, finding quiet places to rest apart from the work he was called to do. Contemplation and soul-work are core practices of the Buddhist and Hindu faiths.

Civil rights activist and poet Maya Angelou writes,

Every person needs to take one day away. A day in which one consciously separates the past from the future. Jobs, family, employers, and friends can exist one day without any one of us, and if our egos permit us to confess, they could exist eternally in our absence. Each person deserves a day away in which no problems are confronted, no solutions searched for. Each of us needs to withdraw from the cares which will not withdraw from us.[2]

Regardless of our vast differences on beliefs most people agree—we need intentional spaces for rest. Like almost everything that matters, rest rarely comes without resistance. In a world and often church that values fast, bigger, and more, rest—real rest—is countercultural. We get so used to filling our time, bellies, hearts, heads, and houses with stuff and things to do that there is little room for quiet, renewal, stillness, and solitude.

We often become so passionate about changing the world (or sometimes just surviving the day) that we forget we need to tend to our own selves first.

As a mother who raised five children and worked full-time for the past fifteen years, I used to scoff at the idea of rest. Rest, really? Give me a break. It just won't work with the demands of my job and All. These. Children. Through time spent with a spiritual director and other faith leaders trying to avoid burnout, I came to realize if I didn't find a way to make room for quiet and spaces to fill my soul, there was no way my body and soul could do this work for the long haul. Just like we hear over the intercom every time we fly on an airplane—we have to put our own oxygen masks on first.

We can't help others if we are barely breathing ourselves.

L'Arche founder Jean Vanier's work is a constant reminder of the value of the simple way, that less is more, slow is good, weakness is strength. We can honor our frail humanity in the mix of being ambassadors of hope. He also cautioned us, "But let us not put our sights too high. We do not have to be saviours of the world! We are simply human beings, enfolded in weakness and in hope, called together to change our world one heart at a time."[3]

One heart at a time.

Sometimes that heart is ours.

There Are a Lot of Ways to Rest

The term *soul care* has become more popular in many circles over the past few years. People have recognized that our fast-paced, consumer-centered culture has definitely taken its toll on people, and there's a need for more inner work to stay the course. However, many have come to associate it with certain specific acts of pampering, like massages and bubble baths, which tend to be available to people with privilege. When I hear people talk about taking time for a bubble bath, it makes me laugh because over half the people I know don't even have houses with bathtubs! Soul care sometimes gets minimized as one small act that requires money or resource in a particular way.

Meaningful soul care is about making sure we are tending to the deepest parts of our experience, that we are grounding ourselves in the roots of God's love, peace, mercy, and hope so we can do the work that we are called to do in the world. The condition of our souls matters. When our souls are exhausted, we can't love well. When we are completely disconnected from our souls, we won't engage from an authentic place. When we are caught up with frantic activity, we won't be present. My friend Julie is a pastor and social worker, working with people experiencing homelessness and insecure housing for years. Just being with Julie is good for my soul, and I love what she recently shared with me: "When I don't rest, when I don't listen to my body and my soul, I live and move in a frantic and reactive mode. Slowing down is what allows my soul to speak, be heard, tended, and followed."

She also helps people consider that listening to our body and soul isn't always about rest that appears quiet or contemplative. Sometimes, she adds, "our souls need time on a punching bag or to go hit the trails on a mountain bike." I really relate to that. Bubble baths aren't my thing, but a fast walk with my dog is. The question that's most important for all of us in the practice of rest is: *What does our unique and tired soul need right now?* That's not always easy to discern, but a start is trying to switch out of a reactive mode into a proactive one—seeking rest in creative ways that work for us.

When it comes to rest (and just about every practice we're discussing), it's crucial not to compare, judge, or evaluate ourselves based on what others are doing. We have to find what works that fits with own personal experiences, resources, circumstances, and desires. For one person, a nap is restful while for another, a brisk hike is. Some like to create alone while others find rest in connection with soul-friends. Extroverts and introverts are filled up in radically different ways.

I truly love the work that I do, and that is one of the factors that makes resting harder. It makes me think of the words of Teresa of Avila, the sixteenth-century Spanish Catholic mystic who says: "Love turns work into rest." When we love what we do, work isn't work and it can often feel like rest. Even though a lot of the work I do is taxing—both emotionally and spiritually—every day I hear a story that fills my soul. Every day I get to see beauty rise from ashes and dignity restored. Every day I witness the tenacity and resilience of the human spirit. But I also need to be more honest with myself—living in the muck and mire of real life takes its toll in places I might not even recognize. No matter how much I love the work, my body, mind, and soul still need rest.

What do you love to do? How can you find a way to do it? For me, anything related to water is deeply healing for me. Water is a life force so I carve out as much time as I can to get on it, by it, in it. Some people would think that the lengths I go to get to water are silly and not at all restful. But to me, it buoys my soul and strengthens my roots so it's always worth the effort.

My friend Phyllis took up pottery a decade ago as a way to heal from her deconstructed faith and find a way to survive being a trauma therapist. I've watched Stacy start kick-boxing, Dave build things, Karen create beautiful jewelry, Sue bike, Heather join a roller derby team, Chris take pictures, John become a student of Reiki, Dawn cook, Jenny paint, Kamla sew, Maggie kayak, and Joy become a yoga instructor. Not everyone has excess money or time, but in their own unique way they all found things they love to do that have become rest for them.

Our Refuge advocates group is dedicated to helping people last in the work of journeying with people in hard places. A focus on soul-care and compassion fatigue is a significant part of our work, and all year long we check in on how we're doing, what we're doing to tend to our souls, and how we are making room for renewal.

Below is a list of soul care practices we have in our Advocates Tool Box:

- Sweat and movement—anything that moves our bodies, exercise, walks, yoga, dance.
- Play—making plans to look forward to and doing some of what we like.
- Creativity—music, poetry, art, nature, beauty.
- Contemplative practices—meditation, prayer, labyrinth walks, silence and solitude.
- Consistent routine—sometimes that means taking prescribed medication on time, eating well, going to bed early.
- Asking for help.
- Sleep!

— Letting go of the message of "I'm not enough"
— Better boundaries and practicing saying "no" when needed.
— Intentional breaks — "I'm just not going to _____" for a while.

What would you add? Which of these are hard for you? Keep considering what you personally need in your soul-care toolbox.

Building a Rhythm of Rest

Over the past few years I have become more drawn to the practices and principles of Celtic Christianity. While there are many streams of Celtic Christian expression, embedded in their broad theology are tenets I deeply resonate with — a value on equality, radical hospitality, contemplative practices, experiencing God in nature, and nonviolence. Add in a belief that the starting place for humans is that we are first and foremost made in the image of God and our work on earth is to draw that out, and I'm sold!

John Philip Newell is one of the leading voices bringing Celtic Christianity to our contemporary culture, and his book *The Rebirthing of God: Christianity's Struggle for New Beginnings* is an excellent faith-centered read. Celtic Christians rely on the natural rhythms of the seasons to guide us, recognizing that they are also reflective of what's going on inside our souls. Newell writes,

> [R]eclaiming the relationship between stillness and action, or between solitude and relationship, is part of the desire to come back into relationship with the wisdom of nature's rhythms. The earth knows its patterns of night followed by day, of winter barrenness succeeded by spring energy and summer fruiting. . . . We know that if we do not give ourselves over to the

darkness and dreaming of nighttime, entering its intimate invitation to sleep and rest, we will only be half-awake to the demands and creativity of the day.[4]

Building a rhythm of rest is participating with the natural cadences of life.

Julie used to work at a rapid pace, juggling ministry, mothering, and working for a local nonprofit. The plates she was spinning are similar to the ones I know a lot of you are juggling. Work, home, life, serving—it's a lot. She was pretty much tired all of the time, tapped out, exhausted, stuck in the grind of life with no relief. She began to recognize that if she kept going at this pace, her heart, soul, and body wouldn't make it. Slowly, surely, she began to make some adjustments to bring a rhythm of rest into her week, month, and year. Making intentional time for silence and solitude, nature, exercise, gardening, and life-giving friends began to tilt things in a different direction. Are things still busy for her? Yes, there's no way around the realities of juggling at this stage of life for her. Yet, her soul is now more grounded and whole as she's embedded a rhythm of rest into her life.

In *The Message* translation of the Bible, the late Eugene Peterson translated Jesus' powerful words in Matthew 11:28–30 this way:

> "Are you tired? Worn out? Burned out on religion? Come to me. Get away with me and you'll recover your life. I'll show you how to take a real rest. Walk with me and work with me—watch how I do it. Learn the unforced rhythms of grace. I won't lay anything heavy or ill-fitting on you. Keep company with me and you'll learn to live freely and lightly."

While often we can interpret that verse as a call to "get away from it all" with God, there's another twist we can add to the mix that my friend Joanna caused me to consider.

When she worked with the most impoverished in India for several years, she did what a lot of us do—created a dichotomy in her mind where rest was only possible outside of her situation. She kept trying to *find rest* by taking breaks from her life. She now shares that she wishes she had learned how to find rest in the middle of the chaos by honoring her soul more tenderly, respecting her needs as an extrovert, and building in more natural rhythms into her daily work than always feeling like she had to "escape" to find rest.

Sabbath Friends

Joanna also calls friends who bring rest to her, "Sabbath friends." These are the kinds of friends who she says are "safe in a place of welcoming, rest, and belonging for my soul." She is one of my Sabbath friends. When I'm with her, I feel centered, grounded, heard, and loved. I can feel my hands and jaw unclench, my body soften, my breath become more even, and peace begin to flow into the places that need it.

Jose and I have some couple friends that bring that same type rest to both of us at the same time. We do not take this gift of soul friendship lightly and do what we can to carve out time to play, laugh, eat, and share our struggles and joys with them. One hundred percent of the time, it's fairly hard to schedule it. We all have busy lives, but we've learned over the years that if we don't make time for connection, it truly won't happen. We also know that every time we leave their presence, we feel better than when we came.

In the Celtic tradition, a term for Sabbath friends is *Anam Cara*, which in Gaelic means soul friend. Ann, a faithful advocate and companion alongside others, says that with soul friends, "Time and distance don't matter, we can always pick up where we left off, and we're always both givers and receivers, one no better or worse than another." This kind of trust and unconditional love in friendship brings a sense of rest and peace to our lives. When we're with soul friends, we can breathe again.

Take a moment to think of your Sabbath or soul friends if you have some. How do they help you experience rest? How can you connect more with them as a regular practice? If you don't have this in your life at the moment but long for it, consider ways you might be able to seek it. Sometimes that starts with connecting with a spiritual director or guide, someone who can help you explore what's going on in your soul right now. Some ways to find one are at the end of this chapter.

Internal Barriers to Rest

A lot of us nod in agreement that these practices of rest are important, but we have strange internal barriers that prevent us from integrating them into our lives. Sometimes what is best for us remain the most elusive. How many of us dread going to the gym, find every excuse we can think of to not go but then once we're there always leave feeling far better than when we came? This is me, almost every single time.

Our internal resistance is something to look at when we think of rest.

Consider some of the internal messages that might be rattling around in your head, barriers to taking good care of your soul and resting:

I am not worthy.
I/we don't have enough money.
I definitely don't have time for that!
If I stop, I'll never start again.
My marginalized friends don't get to rest, why should I?
The world's falling apart, so this is no time for rest!
I feel guilty when I do something for myself.
People will think I'm not working as hard as them if I take a break.

Are any of these messages familiar to you? I hear them a lot from others and say them a lot to myself as well. I can't magically take away these messages, but part of our work is to own that they are getting in the way of health. This is also one of the reasons we need wise supportive people to process with and be accountable to. Left on our own, we will let these messages lead us down the path of exhaustion.

I recently had breakfast with a good friend who cares deeply about social justice issues. We talked about how many good causes there were to join and how distracting it can be. When we are passionate about justice and change, it is easy to want to be part of all the movements — changing oppressive systems, supporting the work of our friends, participating instead of standing on the sidelines.

As he was sharing, a clear and vivid image came to mind of a flowing river. Picture it with me: powerful water, moving, alive, pouring over the rocks, and flowing in the direction it's supposed to flow. Then I saw a bunch of small side streams. Some were bigger than others, and they were pretty, too, winding in all different directions. But those forks didn't have flow. They were side trails that take energy and divert from the primary river. What I noticed is that I often spend so much time on the side streams — all good things — that I can miss out on the real flow.

When it comes to sustaining as people of practice, we need to be careful about spending energy in too many different directions. All of us are probably connected to organizations who care about justice, people who are cultivating amazing things in the world, artists creating beauty and hope, activists working to change laws, and spiritual leaders curating contemplative spaces and conversations we may want to be part of. These things are all good. If you're a parent, you know there are a thousand committees you could join for your kids' school or teams.

But I can't go with all the flows.

Each person's flow is different, and there are good questions we can ask ourselves — What's part of the flow and what isn't? What do we have enough margin and energy for? What's realistic and what isn't? What's the direction I'm supposed to be going and what's just a detour?

Part of the practice of resting is refraining from going with all the flows and spending our energy in the places we know we're supposed to be. We cannot do everything.

When I was in middle school, my mom started going to Al-Anon, the Twelve Step group for those who are in relationship with an addict or alcoholic. I remember the 1970s' garage sale plaque of the Serenity Prayer commonly used in recovery meetings and attributed to Reinhold Niebuhr that she hung on the wall in our house, and it's become one of the most meaningful prayers to me. The short version says:

> God, grant me the serenity to accept the things
>   I cannot change;
> courage to change the things I can;
> and wisdom to know the difference.

In the practice of rest, it is key to acknowledge what's ours to carry and what's not. This can be tricky work, especially for those who struggle with codependency, which is an unhealthy connection with others that manifests through caretaking, control, people-pleasing, and low self-esteem. Knowing what's ours, what's someone else's, can be extremely confusing, especially when our worth depends on being needed.

My friend Mary is a single mom who has been raising four young adults on her own for the past few years. It's hard and tiring work and often difficult to discern where she needs to step in and help them and where she needs to do what's usually the hardest thing to do—let go. When she entered recovery a few years ago, though, she did learn the value of the Serenity Prayer and acknowledging what was in her control and what wasn't.

Like most of us when we get honest, Mary discovered there were far more things out of her control than within it.

What are things we truly can change? Our own thoughts, beliefs, and actions.

What are things we cannot? Others' thoughts, beliefs, and actions.

Accepting that leads to rest, and I've watched Mary and so many friends and fellow strugglers grow as we learn to practice the Serenity Prayer in our own unique ways.

But the World Is Falling Apart

The past several years in the United States have been a problematic and polarizing time for a lot of people. Carrying the reality of ongoing community trauma, the onslaught of a president who tweets daily negativity, and so many people I care about devastated by what's happening politically related to immigration, health care, reproductive justice, and educational policies, it's been a rough season. People who weren't active in civic engagement before are now launching letter-writing campaigns, showing up at political rallies, and community organizing in ways they hadn't before. There's a sense of urgency, an intense feeling of *I've got to do something. I can't just stand by* that has pervaded so many people I know.

When the world's falling apart, it's hard to think about rest.

My husband is an airline pilot, so we get free flights and travel a lot with our family. Over the past few years, we've been on fun adventures to other countries at the same time as bombings, shootings, and other domestic and international trauma. It's always a strange paradox. How can we be enjoying ourselves, laughing, smiling, posting pictures on Facebook when the world is falling apart? There's something that just doesn't feel right about it.

But here's what we keep learning—we can't be constantly available, constantly *on*, constantly connected to each and every painful situation. We need to take breaks, to rest, and do whatever we can do to last. The tricky circumstances are going to be there when we plug back in. There are others who will carry the torch in our absence. Sometimes, the best contribution we can make to a painful event is rest so that when we get back, we are energized and ready to engage.

Steve Knight works on the frontlines of a national community organizing movement dedicated to healing the underlying systemic issues of poverty, racism, and oppression in our country. This team gives their life to social change and rest is often not on their radar. Yet, Steve is learning that without it, he's toast. He shares that this powerful cultural pressure to go, go go, work, work, work—even for things of God—is not the Jesus way. "Jesus taught us and showed us that going away for prayer, even while people were clamoring for healing, was desperately needed." Steve began engaging in contemplative practices like centering prayer and solitude and silence, unplugging from the frenzy and finding a way to ground in a deeper peace and strength that won't come without intention. He, along with so many people I know, are exhausted, weary, and overwhelmed by the work but know that the only way to last is to seek rest.

When the world is falling apart, it's even more important that we find a way to last. The planet and its people need us to be healthy and grounded, not gasping for breath.

In the middle of tangible engagement in the tangled, unpredictable, and beautiful mess of real life and the brokenness of the world, there is peace. There is hope. There is good. Part of the practice of rest is remembering this, to anchor into deeper truths, and recognize we aren't alone in the hard. There are many who have gone before us and many who will go after us. Anne Lamott always helps with a little perspective. She reminds us, "In 100 years? All new people."[5] We are only one part of the big story, and it's important to right-size ourselves in the bigger story.

Our current work is to do what we can to last, to be as healthy, integrated, and grounded as we can be and give ourselves room to fail at resting and keep finding ways to get better at it. This poem by Wendell Berry is one of my favorites and always brings rest to my soul.

Read through it a few times and see what words resonate today.

Peace at Wild Things

When despair for the world grows in me
and I wake in the night at the least sound
in fear of what my life and my children's lives might be,
I go and lie down where the wood drake
rests in his beauty on the water, and the great heron feeds.
I come into the peace of wild things
who do not tax their lives with forethought
of grief. I come into the presence of still water.
And I feel above me the day-blind stars
waiting with their light. For a time
I rest in the grace of the world, and am free.[6]

May you rest in the grace of the world today and be free.

We have one more practice together and it's one of my favorites—celebrating. Rest up, we've got some parties to throw, stories to honor, and celebrating to consider. Like rest, it's what keeps us going.

PRAYER FOR REST

God, we get tired, weary, overwhelmed, exhausted.
Help us rest.
Rest our souls, bodies, minds, hearts.
May the embers that need igniting strengthen us.
May we keep finding peace in the wild things.
Amen.

FOR PERSONAL REFLECTION

1. What makes it hard for you to rest?
2. What are some things you love to do, that bring you life and joy? How are you nurturing more of those things in your life?
3. Read the Serenity Prayer again. What are some things you can't change in your life right now? What can you change?
4. What are some distractions to the flow of your life, things you are doing you know aren't in your primary stream? Can you consider transitioning out of them?

FOR GROUP REFLECTION

1. Pause and notice how your body and soul feel right now. What words come to mind? Share these aloud together.
2. Which of the "Internal Barriers to Rest" messages do you identify with? What else would you add?

3. What are some things you love to do that are restful to your soul? How are you nurturing more of these things in your life? How can group members help one another to incorporate more rest into your lives?
4. Consider the Serenity Prayer, using these prompts. Take a few minutes for everyone to write their reflections before sharing.

> *God, grant me the serenity to accept* _____
>   (things you cannot change)
> *Courage to change the things I can, like* _____
>   (things you can change)
> *And the wisdom to know the difference.*

5. Read the "Peace of Wild Things" out loud in *lectio divina* format (where slowly, you read the text three times, each time noticing what words or phrases or feelings emerge). Share them with the group.

TO PRACTICE

1. Do something that's restful for you—whatever it is. Practice it. Make it happen this week.
2. Think of some of the things that others do for rest that you haven't tried before. Try one of them.
3. Unclutter your mind. What are all the things that are weighing you down? Use these prompts to help you:

> *Right now my heart is heavy with . . .*
> *Things that are beyond my control are . . .*
> *I feel overwhelmed by . . .*
> *I want to let go of . . .*

4. Make time with your Sabbath or soul friend. If you don't have one, begin nurturing a more intentional relationship with someone who could possibly become one for you.

DIG DEEPER

Consolations: The Solace, Nourishment, and Underlying Meaning of Everyday Words by David Whyte

Everything Belongs: The Gift of Contemplative Prayer by Richard Rohr

Permission to Rest: How to Cultivate a Life of Self-Care, Rejuvenation and Nurturing the Spirit by Debra Mae White

Sabbath as Resistance: Saying No to the Culture of Now by Walter Brueggemann

Spiritual Directors International, www.sdiworld.org. This international directory of spiritual directors is a good resource to search for a guide who will help strengthen your soul.

CHAPTER 10

_____

THE PRACTICE OF
CELEBRATING

Cel·e·brate—sel-uh-breyt
Verb / present participle: **celebrating**
1. To publicly honor events or experiences
2. To remember important milestones in creative ways
3. To acknowledge successes and positive movements

> *Throwing parties, sharing stories, finding hope,*
> *practicing the ways of Jesus as best we can.*
> —A Refuge tagline

When our son Jared was about thirteen years old, he developed an addiction to a specific video game. We never let our kids use any electronics Monday through Friday, but come the weekend, that kid could seriously play. We weren't overly concerned about it because it was limited to the weekends, but we expressed hope that he could learn a little better self-control. One morning, completely independent of us, he shared that he was ready to go cold turkey on playing; he recognized he was in trouble when he started setting his alarm to get up early and play. We were so proud of him!

When he had about thirty days without playing anymore, we asked him if we could do what we do for other friends at The Refuge who are working on sobriety from drugs, alcohol, and other addictions—celebrate it together with special chips that honor these changes. Yes, we celebrated at church a thirteen-year-old giving up *Call of Duty*. It was so fun. Everyone loved it, supporting and encouraging him. It was a good marker and public pronouncement of his intention, an example for all ages, and a memory we will always treasure. Yes, every positive movement in the human experience is worth celebrating!

Every positive movement in the human experience is worth celebrating.

In a world that's hard and in need of tender loving care, we sometimes miss the practice of celebrating. We become so focused on what *isn't* that we forget the good that *is*. We forget to make time and space for parties and other celebrations and honor the diverse and wonderful ways we are all transforming. Like the practice of resting, celebrating will help us last in the long game of being more engaged, present, and justice-and-mercy-infused people.

Like each of these practices, what I share here are only ideas. I hope you can integrate the big concepts into your particular contexts, adapt what you need to, and bring them to life and practice in whatever ways work for you and/or your group.

There is no question that living a more connected life—to ourselves, God, and others—is challenging work. Often, we spend so much energy trying to heal our own wounds and the wounds in the world that we get into a kind of *grit our teeth and white knuckle it* mode where life becomes only about whatever we have to do next. We miss the joy. We miss the love. We miss the light. We miss the good.

Often, we're just too darn serious all the time.

I get it. Reality is often heavy and of course I never want to minimize the depth of pain in the world. In some of our Christian experiences we were taught that we needed to take the things of God seriously; that a lot was on the line. It's made for many hard-working, dedicated groups and churches with sincere hearts but with not very much spark and fun. In doing God's work, we can forget to honor and celebrate it.

In the Old Testament, which is shared by both the Jewish and Christian traditions, there are countless festivals that honor different movements of life—ways for people to hold space for God's work in the world and the practices of a faithful life—harvest, freedom from captivity, provision, forgiveness of debts, new seasons. Jose and I recently traveled to Taiwan with two of our young adult children and learned more about the Taiwanese culture. Embedded in Taiwanese life are countless vibrant and special celebrations, all with specific rituals (and food, of course). These set-apart ways to celebrate collectively make a difference. They bind humans together, inspire hope, and catalyze good.

Typically, when we scale through the most common spiritual disciplines we think of silence, solitude, fasting, prayer, worship, and service. The intent of each of these is to somehow deepen our connection with God. While I value these in different ways, I think we're missing a really important one—*celebrations and parties as a core spiritual discipline*. I've written and spoken about it over the years, and each time people really resonate with the idea that celebration and parties are missing from the spiritual disciplines list. I think it's because many people no longer connect (or maybe never did) with some of the more popular and traditional spiritual disciplines. They are too formal, and intense, and we long for something we can integrate into our daily rhythms of life, threading an awareness of God's presence into our here and now no matter what we believe.

Celebration and parties remind us of God's work in our lives and bind us to one another in a myriad of ways.

Jesus Loved a Good Party

Jesus is sometimes portrayed as being extremely solemn, but this is a big misconception. A few clear things we know about him from the four Gospels is that he loved children (who undoubtedly inspire laughter and joy) and went to a lot of parties. Jesus definitely loved a good party! Over and over again, he went to people's houses to eat with diverse groups of folks, attended weddings where water became wine, and hosted outdoor picnics where loaves and fishes were multiplied. A lot happens at community gatherings and parties where people have an opportunity to eat together, laugh, play, drop our guard, and find our shared humanity.

Give me a reason to throw a party for someone, and I'm always in. I love to throw parties! Ever since I was a kid I've been the one planning the get-togethers, hosting the shower, somehow finding a reason to gather people to celebrate something that needs celebrating. Not everyone loves to plan parties, but most people like to participate in them in some shape or form. My awesome teammate at The Refuge Café and in the life of our community, Marrty, has caught the celebrating bug. Before, he left the parties to me, but now he calls me and says, "Hey, I'll pick up a cake to celebrate _____ at the Café this week!" It always makes me smile. Celebrating is contagious.

If you're an introvert you might be cringing right now, thinking how much you *don't* like parties and celebrations! Even though I'm a tried and true extrovert, I honor you. We need all of us. There are big-crowd people and smaller-crowd people, gourmet foodies and premade Costco food junkies (that's me), kids or no-kids types, alcohol or sodas, music or no music types, and a host of other differences that are important to value.

Regardless of preferences, it's good to find ways to get together with other people and honor life. It's why throughout a range of cultures, socioeconomics, and other factors, people find ways to celebrate birthdays, anniversaries, graduations, retirements, promotions, deaths, house-warmings, baby showers, weddings, and other milestones in our lives. Each time we are together for one of these celebrations we are participating in sacred space—no matter how fancy or unintentional.

Every party or celebration is a beautiful form of communion, a celebration of life, an openness to the wind of the Spirit of God into our lives individually and collectively. Each moment is a chance to honor our connectedness to God and to each other.

It Starts with Us

Like all of these practices, it's easy to focus on other people and not ourselves. We would all much rather give than receive, be the helper than the one being helped, the one offering affirmations to others rather than receiving them ourselves.

When it comes to the practice of celebrating, my challenge to all of us is to celebrate the movement we're making in our own lives first. For most of us, this is far harder to do. Years ago, I formed a women's group called the Ex-Good-Christian-Women. The reason we have this name is that all of us somehow no longer fit into the traditional and narrow Christian roles we had been consigned to for many years. We meet once a month and take turns facilitating.

One time, at the end of our semester, I had us walk through an exercise where we had to write down five good things about ourselves. Five. There was so much hemming and hawing, so many "this is so hard!" comments, and all sorts of resistance. The truth is that if each of us were given the same assignment and asked to offer five good things about one another, everyone would be done in a few short minutes. Honoring the good in others comes far more easily than noticing the positive in ourselves.

Part of the practice of celebrating is pausing and owning our own healing, movement, change, and positive shifts in our lives. It starts with us. It helps to look at where we've been, where we are now, what we've overcome, what we've survived, what we've learned, how we've changed. A few months ago I was with my friend Debbie who started the healing path with me over twenty-five years ago. We live in different states now but our bond of friendship has endured the test of time. As we were walking along the beach in San Diego, reflecting on the pain of real life and grieving the recent death of a dear friend, we were reminded that all these years later we're kind of still working on the same core issues. We were also celebrating how much we've grown up and healed through the years and how different our lives look than when we first engaged in the practice of healing.

I'd love for you to pause for a moment and consider your own life and what you'd like to celebrate today. What's changed in you in the past few years? How have you grown? What movement do you need to better honor? What can you celebrate?

All these years later, when I ask my women's group that same type of question — *What's good?* — now there's far less resistance. Positive things come out more naturally, things to celebrate in ourselves emerge more freely. Why? We've been intentionally practicing together.

See What Others Can't See

Writer and speaker Christopher Heuertz has done a lot of work on the Enneagram, a personality tool that many have been using as a pathway for transformation and healing. In his book *The Sacred Enneagram: Finding Your Unique Path to Spiritual Growth,* he reminds us of this important truth: Regardless of our differences, failings, weaknesses, and struggles, "each and every one of us is beautiful. Each and every one of us is beloved by God."[1]

God's image is embedded in each and every human being, no matter our race, religion, sexual identity, age, experience or our mistakes, stumblings, and bumblings. We're all the same that way—made in the image of God. However, the rubble of real life, dysfunctional families, broken relationships, and pain often buries it. The good gets hidden underneath a whole lot of piled-up debris. The light becomes more faint, our true self more hidden. We only see the negative, the hard, the ways we're failing in the world and not living up to our own expectations or what we think others (and sometimes God) expect of us.

We can't see the good.

As people of practice, we can help people see what they can't see for themselves. In the many years I have journeyed with folks, one thing feels pretty consistent—progress can never be measured by others' standards. What is healing for one person is not for another. There's no right or wrong way to experience transformation, and often our focus on a certain kind of outcome for ourselves and others results in completely missing the good.

We make one of the most common mistakes in humanity: *Instead of seeing what is, we only see what isn't.* Can you relate? I do. I can quickly make a long list of the things I need to improve about myself, the goals I haven't met yet, the areas I'm sure I am failing in.

This is why we need each other so desperately. The practice of celebrating is about seeing beyond what's on the surface and celebrating the healing that's happening underneath and might not be as noticeable. This can mean that people still live outside, still have anger and shame from a divorce, still suffer from the ravages of sexual abuse, still drink too much, still are bad with money, still yell at their kids at the grocery store, still are doing things that annoy us. Yet, because we're in relationship with each other, we also know that now they can call a friend when they need help, show up when they want to isolate, share out loud how they're trying to be a safer parent, and are truly trying to do things differently.

On the surface, sometimes the change is imperceptible. This is why we need each other so desperately. We need people who can see what we can't see. We need to be eyes for others, people who remind others of the truth they are experiencing, who celebrate the good, no matter how small or seemingly insignificant. Rob Bell says it well, "If you keep telling people who they are, who their best selves are, if you keep reminding them of their true identity, there's a good chance they'll figure out what to do."[2]

When I first met Kamla she was in her early twenties and trying to heal from a myriad of abusive relationships in her family and church. She moved to another state so we lost touch for a few years. When she re-entered my life she had recently been released from a short stint in jail, and her husband had just killed himself. She pretty much could barely breathe and was trying to survive those initial months of grief. With no high school diploma, marketable job skills, or safe people in her life, she slowly and surely forged forward. It's been a bumpy ride, and one of the hardest things for her to believe is that there's anything good in her. She's used to being mistreated, abandoned, rejected, and she often intersects with the world that way, coming across hard and harsh when the truth is she's incredibly tender and loving. Underneath her pain is a talented, creative, funny, compassionate, smart, strong, and brave woman who's trying to grow up and break out of her extremely unhealthy family system. I meet with her regularly to remind her of who she really is, the part of Kamla that's hard for Kamla to see. Each and every time, she says almost the same thing: "Kathy, I'm trying to see what you see."

Author Victoria Price says, "What more can any of us do for one another but to retell one another that we are lovely."[3] I can't make Kamla believe the good, but I can keep telling her what I see, that she is lovely. It also helps that others are telling Kamla a similar message, too. Community is where it's at, people.

Finding Things to Celebrate

Embedded into the practice of celebrating is gratitude. Gratitude always heals. There's new mindfulness research coming out that shows that gratitude actually changes the chemistry of our brain in a positive way. In the Twelve Steps of Alcoholic Anonymous, there's an emphasis on cultivating "an attitude of gratitude." There is something very powerful about turning our intentions outward, remembering the good, and acknowledging them, either out loud or in the quiet of our heart. Aletheia Luna and Mateo Sol, in their book *The Power of Solitude*, write, "To experience gratitude is to experience an appreciation of the present moment, of what we possess right now. . . . Gratitude is a gift that centers us firmly in the here and now."[4] Often, we're so focused on the future that we forget to celebrate the present.

The Ignatian Prayer of Daily Examen is centered on creating contemplative space where we notice God's presence in our lives at the end of the day. I sometimes tell people to mix that up and look for some things they are grateful for today, that they want to celebrate, notice, acknowledge. Usually, even when people are in a dark and hard place in their lives and the last thing they want to do is celebrate good, they can come up with at least one thing, even if it's as simple as "my dog" or "I got out of bed." There's always something to be grateful for, and that's part of the practice of celebrating.

What are some things you can celebrate, movement that's being made in yours and other people's lives? How can you honor and acknowledge it?

I was thinking of the past season at The Refuge and some of the things we've held space for, honored, and celebrated in community together: A five-year-old's birthday, a seventy-year-old's birthday (and too many other birthdays to count), a wedding against all odds, sobriety birthdays from drugs and alcohol, friends setting healthy boundaries with in-laws, a free shower, leaving an abusive relationship, an adult adoption for someone with no living family, making it through the holidays, new jobs, finishing school, entering therapy, finding stable housing, starting new dreams. Those are just a few.

It's also important to not only think of what we consider *positive* when we're celebrating.

One of the most beautiful spaces I have ever facilitated as a pastor was an "un-wedding" ceremony for a dear friend. When Amy Jo came out as lesbian after being married for fifteen years, she and her husband tried to find a way to make it work. In the end, it was clear—they needed to end their marriage as husband and wife and transition into the next phase of their relationship as best friends and coparents of their two young daughters. Together we crafted a meaningful celebration where they untied the cords of their marriage and retied them for a different future. Over thirty people and their precious girls witnessed their new sacred vows, celebrated the life they had built, and blessed them for the next chapter of their story.

Some of you might be saying, *What the what? A pastor honoring a divorce publicly, really?* The answer is an emphatic *yes.* It was an honor to hold space for them, and I truly wish more people would consider these kinds of celebrations and holy rituals as a natural part of life together. They help shift something in not only the participant's souls but also all those witnessing it as well. They handled the inevitable end in the most beautiful way possible, and we honored their courage. What's sometimes perceived as a failure can be transformed into a celebration of the good. Honoring life truthfully and publicly removes shame and honors a redemptive story, which we know always includes intense pain. It restores dignity where it can easily be lost in our human tendency to hide. I'm not saying we all have to go around creating un-wedding experiences for those getting a divorce, but my hope is that we will all stretch our imagination on the practice of celebrating beyond only what's perceived as good. We can transform perceived failures into celebrations, too. Imagine how much healing could happen in the world if we embedded more of this kind of celebrating into the fabric of our lives together?

All of our networks are different, but the idea is always the same. Consider the people in your circle, at home, work, school, church, or wherever you live and move. What are some things happening in their lives you can help celebrate?

Celebration as Resurrection

One of my favorite -ing words that didn't make it as its own chapter is resurrecting. Here are a few synonyms for *resurrecting*: *awakening, bouncing back, breathing new life into, brightening, coming to life, making whole, overcoming, reawakening, recovering, rekindling, renewing, renovating, restoring, snapping out of it, springing up, strengthening, waking up.*

All of these words are part of the practice of celebrating. I love humanity's resilience, ways people bounce back, resurrect, come to life, wake up. My hope is that we'd be people who are constantly resurrecting in our own lives and helping others do the same in theirs.

In our own unique ways, many of us are waking up, healing, shedding things that hinder, coming to life again after a season of painful loss, finding our voice and advocating, resisting, persisting, uncovering our passions, discovering life in unlikely places, showing up instead of hiding, thawing hardened hearts, trying new things, loosening our grip on things we once held tightly, trying to stand up after a season of crawling.

The world needs these resurrection stories! We need to hear the good, witness courage, and be inspired. In the midst of the brokenness that's often so much easier to see, these stories of healing, hope, redemption, new life—no matter how small or big—not only help strengthen and encourage us individually but help ignite faith in the good of humanity as well. Writer Thomas Moore asks, "How do you resurrect in your everyday life? You learn to see through the literal all around you to the greater mysteries at work."[5]

Becoming Celebrating People and Celebrating Communities

As we wrap this chapter and come to the end of our time together, there are some specific ways we can become people and communities who practice celebrating. Here are a few ideas:

— *Honor movement in ourselves first.* This isn't ungodly or selfish. It's important to notice what's healing and changing in us as people of practice.
— *Cultivate authentic, meaningful relationships with people.* We can't celebrate what we don't know, and this is why all roads lead to relationship. When we're in relationship with other people, we notice and know what's happening in their lives that we can celebrate together.
— *Resist our tendency to minimize or measure movement.* It's easy to downplay movement by comparing it to others or minimizing. Every little bit of change in our own unique ways is worth honoring!
— *Practice gratitude.* It's the simplest form of celebrating. Embedded into our daily rhythms, it will transform us.
— *Do what works.* Everyone is different. Some like larger gatherings, others like small intimate ones. Not everyone has a big budget. The venue is not

important; the heart and creativity behind it is what matters the most.

When we baptize people, I always love sharing 2 Corinthians 5:17: "The old has gone, the new is here" (NIV). But, in my daily living, I also like to think of new life and resurrecting as an active and ongoing part of spiritual formation and transformation and prefer this phrase for that: *The old is always dying, and the new is always coming.* That's much more what real life is like for most of us.

The old is always dying, the new is always coming.

That's always worth celebrating.

A PRAYER FOR CELEBRATING

God, give us eyes to notice transformation in our own lives and those around us.
From brief prayers of gratitude to big, creative parties,
help us honor and celebrate the good.
Keep reminding us that the old is always dying, the new is always coming.
We want to keep resurrecting.
Amen.

FOR PERSONAL REFLECTION

1. Make a list of some good things that are happening in your life, no matter how big or small. Write them all down. This is a great start on a gratitude list.

2. How do you sometimes minimize movement in your own life by downplaying growth or overlooking personal milestones for celebration?
3. What are some things that people in your life are celebrating? Is there a way you can help acknowledge and honor them?

FOR GROUP REFLECTION

1. On a scale of 1 to 10, 1 being hard and 10 being easy, how do you feel about celebrating? Why? What are some of your experiences with it?
2. Take turns sharing some good things—big or small—that are happening in your life right now: *I'm celebrating. . . .* Share these out loud together.
3. What prevents you from celebrating movement in your own life? What are some of the barriers, the things you say to yourself?
4. Review the synonyms for *resurrecting*: *awakening, bouncing back, breathing new life into, brightening, coming to life, making whole, overcoming, reawakening, recovering, rekindling, renewing, renovating, restoring, snapping out of it, springing up, strengthening, waking up.* What other words for resurrecting would you add? Which feel true for you right now? How are they playing out in your real life?
5. Close your time together with a gratitude list. Go around and share what you're grateful for in a simple sentence.

TO PRACTICE

1. Whenever you notice change in someone's life, share it with them in a specific way. Maybe it's a card, an email, a real-life conversation.
2. Find a reason to throw a party! What needs celebrating and how can you be part of honoring it, no matter how small or big?
3. What is something you would like to celebrate in your life? Reach out to some friends and share and see if there's a way to mark it together.
4. The Daily Examen—consider trying this Ignatian spiritual practice, using some of these prompts as a guide:

Notice God's presence in your day. Where did you feel connection with God, with your soul?

Practice gratitude. Scale through your day and notice what you are thankful for in your day, no matter how seemingly insignificant.

Reflect on your emotions. What were you feeling today? When? Why?

Choose one aspect of your day that you want to pray about, reflect on, contemplate.

Look forward to tomorrow and a new day to practice again.

DIG DEEPER

To Bless the Space between Us: A Book of Blessings by John O'Donohue

The Book of Joy: Lasting Happiness in a Changing World by the Dalai Lama and Desmond Tutu

The Gift of Wonder: Creative Practices for Delighting in God by Christine Aroney-Sine

Grateful: The Subversive Practice of Giving Thanks by Diana Butler Bass

Help, Thanks, Wow: Three Essential Prayers by Anne Lamott

CONCLUSION

Keep Practicing

*Against all odds and past history, we are loved and chosen,
and do not have to get it together before we show up.*
—Anne Lamott[1]

Recently, I did a podcast interview for my friend Matt
Kendziera's podcast *Jesus Never Ran*. It's not centered on
anything related to running for politics, but rather how
things of God are typically slow. Jesus wasn't fast, efficient,
or concerned at all with "excellence" or "performance." In
fact, what he embodied was anything but. Words I'd probably use to describe a lot of what we know about Jesus'
ways in the Gospels include *strange, awkward*, and *confusing*.
In the podcast, I shared how one of the most important
things I've learned over twenty-five years of slogging in the
trenches with my own soul work and the heart and guts of
others is how freaking long real transformation takes.

I never measure things in days, weeks, months or even
several years anymore.

Deep transformation is lengthy, and sometimes this is tough for people to accept. When asked how long personal, emotional, or practical change might take or why I don't see people moving forward fast enough for some others' liking, I often say *give it a decade.*

A decade? Wait, what?

That's not very encouraging. I am guessing when you started reading this book you were expecting a little more speed.

I hear you, and truly believe if we all start practicing some of what we've been engaging with together that we will, indeed, see change far sooner than that. Our lives will feel more connected and integrated, our hearts more engaged, our hands and feet more active in loving and living in ways that make a difference. Hopefully, we'll get to taste some of the fruit here, now.

However, part of being healthier people of practice in the world is also acknowledging more honestly that we won't be able to topple systems of inequality quickly or become a master at holding space for differing views overnight or all of a sudden wake up completely healed from some of the patterns we've been used to doing in our lives for years.

This is why I always come back to the original word *practice* and its focus on repetition, intention, and ongoing improvement.

Years ago when my oldest son Joshua was in first grade, I homeschooled him for a year and a half (I can safely say I was terrible at homeschooling). It was a worthy experiment but trying to juggle him, my two other preschoolers and two newborn twins wasn't the best idea in the world. That entire season was a bit comical, and I remember some of the struggles he and I had in our basement classroom. Sometimes, when he took a test and didn't get 100 percent, he would get so mad at himself, so mad at me. He was only six years old and no one was looking at his grades. I remember telling him, "Josh, this whole learning thing isn't about getting 100 percent. That's why we call it *school*. It's about learning. We're not supposed to be nailing it all the time."

He wasn't convinced.

However, those words have lingered for me twenty years later because I, too, want to master everything from the very beginning. I want to nail the practices of healing, listening, loving, including, equalizing, advocating, mourning, resting, and celebrating (and completely avoid the failing one).

But when it comes to a life of practice, there are no perfect scores to shoot for, no A+'s to earn, no accolades to receive.

We are going to bring our beautiful, flawed, amazing, neurotic, tired, and energized selves to play over and over again as we open our hearts and experiences to practicing, falling, learning, crawling, and trying to live a more embodied life in a fragmented world.

It's so good to accept our limitations and remember we're just learners. There's no reason to get mad at ourselves when we screw up in relationship, are terrible listeners, get called out on our lack of awareness about race, fail to always use gender-inclusive language, or burn out and need to take an extended break from service. Get ready, because they're all going to happen if they haven't already.

I'm sometimes not only hard on myself but others too. I want people around me to change at exactly the same pace as me because that makes it far easier. I want others to "get" some of these ideas about inclusion, equality, and listening. I want to be able to freely talk about what I'm learning and energized by without people's eyes glazing over.

It can be so lonely and frustrating when we change and others around us don't. When we start advocating for people who others around us don't seem to care about. When we start changing the way we are showing up in the world and friends and family begin to notice and start to wish we hadn't changed because they liked us better when we were quieter, nicer, and less engaged. Over time, I have lost some friends along the way because of some of these practices. These were people I thought I'd be traveling with forever, but when it came to some of these core issues, our relationship just didn't make it through. It's painful to me but I have come to accept that loss is sometimes part of the cost of living out what we deeply value.

When we change, sometimes our relationships do, too.

When how we live out our faith radically shifts, many of our relationships shift, too.

Each of you reading is in a unique place in your story right now. Some of you have been hacking at a more incarnational life for many years now and this book has just been confirmation of what you've already been doing. Others of you are new to some of these ideas and are just now beginning to put your toes in the water to consider what it might be like to jump in.

Whether you consider yourself a follower of Jesus or not, a life of changing ourselves to change the world is going to be a bumpy, windy, weird road. We will have good and bad days, better and worse seasons. Some days we will feel inspired and clear and other days we will wake up wanting to run for the hills and never see another human or turn on the television again.

We will stumble and bumble as we practice. We will make mistakes. We will look stupid. We will doubt ourselves. We will be irritated with others. We will wonder if it's all worth it.

I've no doubt that a life of practice is worth every bit of blood, sweat, tears, guts, and heart we put into it over our lifetime. We are meant to be in relationship. We are meant to embody a better way. We are meant to be the hands and feet of Jesus in a world that's crying out for hope — not haggling over Bible verses or theological differences.

We've covered a lot of ground in this book. I am guessing you liked certain chapters more than others, were drawn to particular practices over others, and were challenged by how much there is to work on.

I am right in the thick of practicing along with you. There is so much more that could be said about these ten practices—entire books are written on some of the sections we processed quickly together. My hope, however, is that you would integrate what you could into your own particular stories and contexts and use these ideas and practices in any way that inspires, heals, and helps you continue to live a more free, full, and engaged life in relationship with yourselves and others; that this book would be a springboard for next steps that are practical and tangible.

We learned that the starting place for embodying change is by working on our own healing, acknowledging unhealthy patterns, and continuing to grow personally. We can't ask people to go where we're not willing to travel ourselves first. In a fractured and divided world, we focused on the practice of listening, learning about dignified dialogue, embracing a life of more ears, less mouth, and building bridges across big divides instead of bombing them. Loving is the heart of our faith and practice, yet it's no easy task and can never be mastered—we're bankrupt without it. We considered ways we could love more fully, not only our neighbors but also God and ourselves.

The practices of including and equalizing went hand in hand as we engaged with how much work we have to do to break down walls, expand our tables, and shift power in our unhealthy, oppressive systems. Our participation in this is crucial as inclusion and equality won't come without rocking the boat and disrupting the status quo. That always starts with us and examining our own power and privilege and living with that discomfort. Then we explored how the practice of advocating is much more than writing letters to government officials but instead living a life of *with*-based incarnational living alongside others in reciprocal relationship where we all give and we all receive. We all need an advocate, and we can all be one.

Another part of moving differently in the world is being people who engage in the practice of mourning, allowing ourselves and others to feel hard feelings without shutting them down or relieving our own anxiety. Some of these losses we are grieving and processing can make us feel like failures, and the practice of failing helps us remember our humanity and that there's no such thing as "failing" but only opportunities to continue to grow and smash shame and cultivate resilience.

We also delved into the practice we all want to skip over because we're so busy practicing: resting. Even though the world is falling apart and there's never enough time, we must find ways to still our minds, bodies, and souls, and find rest. We must. We need to last! And we won't unless we nurture creative spaces to clear the clutter and anchor in peace so we can last over the long haul.

Lastly, we looked at the practice of celebrating and how throwing parties and being people of gratitude is desperately needed to stay the course. There's always something to celebrate and gratitude always heals. Each baby step adds up over time, and every small movement matters.

I'd love for each of you to consider where you've been since you started *Practicing*. What was stirred up in you? Where were you encouraged? Challenged? Disrupted? Healed? What resonated? What would you have added? What do you want to keep engaging with more deeply?

I wish we could be in the same room together to process some of your reflections, but the next best thing is hearing what got stirred up in you through *Practicing*. I love getting messages and hearing the good, the bad, and the ugly. It's also helpful if you can share it out loud with someone in your current circle in real life. Let them know what you're trying, learning, and what's shifting inside of you. If you don't have anyone in this moment, my hope is always that somehow, some way, you can find some kindred spirits who are traveling on the path of a more engaged life of practice also. There are so many people who are done with going to church and want to be the church, who aren't sure what they believe but know they believe in love and want to be part of changing the world, who are faithful followers of Jesus and want to talk about his wild and beautiful ways with others who are practicing too. I know sometimes they're hard to find, but I hope you can.

My daughter, Julia, is currently in dental school, so it won't be long until we have a Dr. Escobar in the family. She's worked her tail off to get where she is today. My husband Jose and I have also worked passionately on our relationship not only with Julia but all of our kids over the years, untangling from some of the unhealthy parenting skills we employed early on when we were in a rigid faith system. We talk freely about healing from some of the bad theological constructs we embedded into her and our work to shift our family from being shame-based to becoming healthier, freer, and more integrated. I am ever grateful for the long haul work we all did together to get to a new place over the years. When Julia was visiting from New York City over her spring break, she paused in one of our conversations and said, "Mom, I want to tell you something. Thank you for changing. You and dad have changed so much over the years and I am so freaking grateful."

I will also always treasure a story one of Jared's friends shared at his memorial service. While on a hike a few months before he died, he told her, "I don't' know what I believe about Christianity, but my mom's a badass."

For this broken mama's heart, that was pure gold.

If we had stayed in our comfortable, protected, rigid Christian bubble, I honestly don't know where we'd be today. Both Julia and Jared's words mean the world to me because they signify that our kids experienced something different in us over the years. Practicing some of these unfamiliar ways hasn't been pretty or smooth, and it most certainly hasn't been easy.

But I know one thing for sure—it's been totally worth it.

Practicing the ways of healing, listening, loving, including, equalizing, advocating, mourning, failing, resting, and celebrating are *totally worth it.*

You are too.

And so is the world. It deserves better and we can be part of making it that way.

As we close, please know this—my stumbling, bumbling, learning, practicing, dreaming, trying-to-always-stay-open heart is always with you from afar.

It's an honor to keep practicing together.

A PRAYER FOR PRACTICING

God, we need your courage to keep practicing.
Help us stay the course when we want to give up.
Stir our hearts, move our feet, rock our world.
We're ready, we're willing, we're open.
Help us keep changing ourselves so we can change the world.
Amen.

FOR PERSONAL REFLECTION

1. Look back and consider what journeying through this material was like for you? What shifted in you? How were you challenged, inspired, or disrupted?
2. Consider the ten practices we covered—healing, listening, loving, including, equalizing, advocating, mourning, failing, resting, and celebrating. Which do you want to go back to and explore more right now? Which chapter was the hardest for you? Why?

3. What's a next challenge for you, something or someone you know you want to engage with in the weeks
   and months to come in a tangible way?
4. If you want, write your own prayer or intention,
   moving forward.

> *God, I want to keep* _____ (things
> you want to keep learning about, practicing,
> trying)
> *I'm inspired to* _____ (dreams or chal-
> lenges that you want to explore)
> *I'm scared of* _____ (fears or anxieties)
> *I'm excited to* _____ (new things you
> want to try)
> *Help me* _____ (ways you need God's
> or others' help)

FOR GROUP DISCUSSION

1. As a group, go back through the highlights of the
   ten practices—healing, listening, loving, including,
   equalizing, advocating, mourning, failing, resting,
   and celebrating. What lingered? Which were the
   hardest for you? What do you want to go back and
   consider more in the weeks and months to come?
2. If you tried some of the practices at the end of each
   chapter, share with the group what your experience
   was like. What did you learn? What does it prompt
   you to consider?
3. If you used the prayer prompt from the Personal
   Reflection section, share it with the group.
4. What's next for you? Is there something *Practicing*
   stirred up in you that you want to keep cultivating
   in your life in a more intentional way? Share with

the group, even if your idea is still unformed. It's good to say these things out loud. There is power in speaking your truth.

5. Consider your time as a group over the past season. What did you love about your experience together? What did you learn from each other? What do you want to celebrate? What do you want to keep practicing together as a community?

TO PRACTICE

1. *Be creative.* Make some your own practices, things you know you want to try, do, explore. Take any of the ideas you've learned and expand on them in ways that work for your unique story.
2. *Be brave.* Consider what is stirring up in you and try to take a step toward it, no matter how big or small.
3. *Be a learner.* Read some of the books or resources in the Dig Deeper sections. Attend workshops on some of these difficult topics, keep exploring more.
4. *Be gentle with yourself.* Remember, we're all stumbling and bumbling together, and it's so important we offer ourselves and others grace.
5. *Be.* Yes, the world is broken and there's a lot of work to be done, but find a way to rest, to laugh, to lighten the load, to see the good in the present.

And because we always need to be reminded, the last words in this book will be the first words we started with in this chapter from Anne Lamott.

Against all odds and past history, we are loved and chosen, and do not have to get it together before we show up.

NOTES

Chapter 1: The Practice of Healing

1. William Paul Young, "How to Actually Help People Who Are Hurting," http://wmpaulyoung.com/how-to-actually-help-people-who-are-hurting, accessed May 26, 2019.

2. Brené Brown, *The Gifts of Imperfection: Let Go of Who You Think You're Supposed to Be and Embrace Who You Are* (Center City, MN: Hazeldon Publishing, 2010), xiv.

3. Brown, *The Gifts of Imperfection*, 20.

4. Richard Rohr, *Breathing Under Water: Spirituality and the Twelve Steps* (Cincinnati, OH: St. Anthony Messenger Press, 2011), xxi.

5. Henri Nouwen, "The Wounded Healer," https://henrinouwen.org/meditation/the-wounded-healer, accessed May 25, 2019.

Chapter 2: The Practice of Listening

1. Lonni Collins Pratt, *Radical Hospitality: Benedict's Way of Love* (Brewster, MA: Paraclete Press, 2011), 120.

2. International Listening Association, https://www.listen.org, accessed April 15, 2018.

3. Mark Nepo, *Seven Thousand Ways to Listen: Staying Close to What Is Sacred* (New York: Free Press, 2012), 37.

4. Parker J. Palmer, *A Hidden Wholeness: The Journey toward an Undivided Life* (San Francisco: Jossey-Bass, 2004), 130.

5. Palmer, *A Hidden Wholeness*, 123.

Chapter 3: The Practice of Loving

1. Coleman Barks, *A Year with Rumi: Daily Readings* (New York: HarperCollins, 2006), 197.

2. Richard Rohr (@RichardRohrOFM), "The best criticism of the bad is the practice of the better," Twitter, August 27, 2014, https://twitter.com/richardrohrofm/status/504733911629701120.

3. Henri J. M. Nouwen, *Life of the Beloved: Spiritual Living in a Secular World* (New York: Crossroad, 1992), 45.

4. Brian McLaren, *Author's Commentary to We Make the Road by Walking: A Year-Long Quest for Spiritual Formation, Reorientation, and Activation*, https://brianmclaren.net/wp-content/uploads/2016/10/wmtr -commentary.pdf.

5. Danielle Shroyer, *Original Blessing: Putting Sin in Its Rightful Place* (Minneapolis: Fortress Press, 2016), xi.

6. Thich Nhat Hanh, *Your True Home: The Everyday Wisdom of Thich Nhat Hanh* (Boston: Shambhala, 2011), chap. 15.

7. Kathy Escobar, *Down We Go: Living into the Wild Ways of Jesus* (Folsom, CA: Civitas Press, 2011), 77.

8. Jean Vanier, *Community and Growth*, 2nd rev. ed. (Mahwah, NJ: Paulist Press, 1989), 298.

Chapter 4: The Practice of Including

1. Brandan Robertson, *True Inclusion: Creating Communities of Radical Embrace* (St. Louis: Chalice Press, 2018), 3.

2. John Pavlovitz, *A Bigger Table: Building Messy, Authentic, and Hopeful Spiritual Community* (Louisville, KY: Westminster John Knox Press, 2017), 30–31.

3. Rachel Held Evans, *Inspired: Slaying Giants, Walking on Water, and Loving the Bible Again* (Nashville: Thomas Nelson, 2018), 186.

4. Tram Nguyen, ed., *"Language Is a Place of Struggle": Great Quotes by People of Color* (Boston: Beacon Press, 2009), 89.

5. René Girard, *Violence and the Sacred*, trans. Patrick Gregory (Baltimore: Johns Hopkins University Press, 1977).

Chapter 5: The Practice of Equalizing

1. Austin Channing Brown, *I'm Still Here: Black Dignity in a World Made for Whiteness* (New York: Convergent, 2018), 171.

2. Margaret J. Wheatley, *Turning to One Another: Simple Conversations to Restore Hope to the Future* (San Francisco: Berrett-Koehler, 2002), 75.

3. James Baldwin, "Faulkner and Desegregation," *Partisan Review*, 23, no. 4 (1956): 568–73.

4. Peggy McIntosh, "What Is White Privilege," https://www.whiteprivilegeconference.com/what-is-white-privilege, accessed February 15, 2019.

5. Robin J. DiAngelo, *White Fragility: Why It's So Hard for White People to Talk about Racism* (Boston: Beacon Press, 2018), 2.

6. DiAngelo, *White Fragility*, 2.

7. "Papal Bull Dum Diversas 18 June, 1452" Doctrine of Discovery, updated July 23, 2018, http://www.doctrineofdiscovery.org/dum-diversas/.

8. Craig Greenfield, *Subversive Jesus: An Adventure in Justice, Mercy, and Faithfulness in a Broken World* (Grand Rapids: Zondervan, 2016), 18.

Chapter 6: The Practice of Advocating

1. Dorothy Day, *The Reckless Way of Love: Notes on Following Jesus*, ed. Carolyn Kurtz (Walden, NY: Plough Publishing, 2017), 67.

2. MT Dávila, "To Know What Christian Activism Looks Like, Make a Friend," *Daily Theology*, May 3, 2017, https://dailytheology.org/2017/05/03/to-know-what-christian-activism-looks-like-make-a-friend.

3. Mark Votava, *The Mystical Imagination: Seeing the Sacredness of All of Life* (Portland, OR: Urban Loft Publishers, 2015), chap. 12, Kindle.

4. Brené Brown, *Rising Strong: How the Ability to Reset Transforms the Way We Live, Love, Parent, and Lead* (New York: Random House, 2015), chap. 9.

Chapter 7: The Practice of Mourning

1. Rob Bell and Don Goldman, *Jesus Wants to Save Christians: Learning to Read a Dangerous Book* (New York: HarperOne, 2012), chap. 2.

2. Henri J. M. Nouwen, *Out of Solitude: Three Meditations on the Christian Life* (Notre Dame, IN: Ava Maria Press, 2004), 38

3. Elisabeth Kübler-Ross, *On Death and Dying: What the Death and Dying Have to Teach Doctors, Nurses, Clergy, and Their Own Family* (New York: Macmillan, 1969; repr., New York: Scribner Classics, 1997), 7.

4. Brené Brown, *Rising Strong: How the Ability to Reset Transforms the Way We Live, Love, Parent, and Lead* (New York: Random House, 2015), chap. 2.

5. Parker J. Palmer, *A Hidden Wholeness: The Journey toward an Undivided Life* (San Francisco: Jossey-Bass, 2004), 178.

6. Palmer, *A Hidden Wholeness*, 181.

7. Phileena Heuertz, *Mindful Silence: The Heart of Christian Contemplation* (Downers Grove, IL: InterVarsity Press, 2018), chap. 4.

8. Hope Edelman, *Motherless Daughters: The Legacy of Loss* (Reading, MA: Addison-Wesley, 1994; repr., Boston: Da Capo Lifelong, 2014), 5.

9. Teresa B. Pasquale, *Sacred Wounds: A Path to Healing from Spiritual Trauma* (St. Louis: Chalice Press, 2015), chap. 7.

10. Francis Weller, "The Geography of Sorrow: An Interview with Francis Weller on Navigating Our Losses," interview by Tim McKee, *Sun Magazine*, October 2015, https://thesunmagazine.org/issues/478/the-geography-of-sorrow.

Chapter 8: The Practice of Failing

1. Lin-Manuel Miranda, *Gmorning, Gnight: Little Pep Talks for Me and You* (New York: Random House, 2018), 10.

2. Henri J. M. Nouwen, *Can You Drink the Cup?* (Notre Dame, IN: Ave Maria Press, 1996; rev. ed. 2006), 54.

3. Brené Brown, *Rising Strong: How the Ability to Reset Transforms the Way We Live, Love, Parent, and Lead* (New York: Random House, 2015), introduction.

4. Anne Lamott, *Bird by Bird: Some Instructions on Writing and Life* (New York: Pantheon, 1994; repr., South Shore, MA: Anchor Press, 2007), 35.

5. Susan David, *Emotional Agility: Get Unstuck, Embrace Change, and Thrive in Work and Life* (New York: Avery, 2016), chap. 2.

6. Sarah Bessey, *Out of Sorts: Making Peace with an Evolving Faith* (New York: Howard Books, 2015), chap. 1.

7. Elizabeth Gilbert, *Big Magic: Creative Living beyond Fear* (New York: Riverhead Books, 2015), 251–52.

8. Miranda, *Gmorning, Gnight*, 11.

Chapter 9: The Practice of Resting

1. Phileena Heuertz, *Mindful Silence: The Heart of Christian Contemplation* (New York: Random House, 1993; repr., Downers Grove, IL: InterVarsity Press, 2018), chap. 1.

2. Maya Angelou, *Wouldn't Take Nothing for My Journey Now* (New York: Random House, 1993; repr., New York: Bantam Books, 2011), 139.

3. Jean Vanier, *Becoming Human* (Mahweh, NJ: Paulist Press, 1998), v.

4. John Philip Newell, *The Rebirthing of God: Christianity's Struggle for New Beginnings* (Woodstock, VT: Skylight Paths, 2014), chap. 5.

5. Anne Lamott, *All New People* (Berkeley, CA: Counterpoint, 1989), chap. 5.

6. Wendell Berry, "Peace of Wild Things," in *The Selected Poems of Wendell Berry* (Berkeley, CA: Counterpoint, 2009), 43.

Chapter 10: The Practice of Celebrating

1. Christopher L. Heuertz, *The Sacred Enneagram: Finding Your Unique Path to Spiritual Growth* (Grand Rapids: Zondervan, 2017), chap. 1.

2. Rob Bell, *What Is the Bible? How an Ancient Library of Poems, Letters, and Stories Can Transform the Way You Think and Feel about Everything* (New York: HarperOne, 2017), chap. 6.

3. Victoria Price, *The Way of Being Lost: A Road Trip to My Truest Self* (Mineola, NY: Ixia Press, 2018), chap. 22.

4. Aletheia Luna and Mateo Sol, *The Power of Solitude* (Australia: LonerWolf, 2016), chap. 4.

5. Thomas Moore, *A Religion of One's Own: A Guide to Creating a Personal Spirituality in a Secular World* (New York: Gotham Books, 2014), chap. 6.

Conclusion

1. Anne Lamott, *Help, Thanks, Wow: The Three Essential Prayers* (New York: Riverhead Books, 2012), 5.